Mnemotechnics
The Art and Science of Memory Techniques

M.A. KOHAIN

Copyright © 2016 M.A. Kohain

All rights reserved.
ISBN: 1536985244
ISBN-13: 978-1536985245

Table of Contents

Preface 1
Part 1 | What is the Purpose of Memory? 3
Part 2 | How are Memories Formed? 7
Part 3 | The Art of Memory 11
Part 4 | Mnemonic Devices 15
Part 5 | Thirty Two Methods for Acquiring Images to Represent Words 19
Part 6 | The First Alphabet 26
Part 7 | The Second Alphabet 33
Part 8 | The Method of Loci 40
Part 9 | Sequence, Order, and Category 57
Part 10 | The Method of Loci Continued 62
Part 11 | A Small Universe and the Practical Application of the Method of Loci 65
Part 12 | A Major Example 72
Part 13 | For Geography 103
Part 14 | Natural Symmetry 114
Part 15 | For Mathematical Equations 118
Part 16 | For the Memorization of Numbers 125
Part 17 | For the Memorization of Poetry, Sentences, and Paragraphs 128
Part 18 | The Method of Loci Applied to Poetry, Sentences, and Paragraphs 131
Part 19 | Paintings and 2-Dimensionality 132
Part 20 | On Sexualization 136

PART 21 | TEMPORAL MNEMONICS AND TEMPORAL LOCI: HOW TO MEMORIZE TIMES, DATES, AND FACTS IN HISTORY 147

PART 22 | ON DETAIL AND IMAGINATION 154

PART 23 | MEMORY WEIGHT 156

PART 24 | SIZE OPTIMIZATION 157

PART 25 | LENGTH, BREADTH, AND WIDTH SPECIFICATION 158

PART 26 | PERSPECTIVE DISJUNCTION 159

PART 27 | OCULAR FIXATION 160

PART 28 | IMAGE SPECIFICATION 161

PART 29 | LOCALIZATION AND DELOCALIZATION 162

PART 30 | DIRECT AND INDIRECT SYMBOLISM 163

PART 31 | RELATIVE ORIENTATION 164

PART 32 | REGARDING ARTIFICIAL MEMORY CITIES ... 165

FINAL NOTE 169

GLOSSARY OF TERMS 170

BIBLIOGRAPHY & FOOTNOTES 174

Preface

Dear Reader,

What is it that you want most from this book? If you want it to supply you multiple ways to improve your ability memorize and recall information, then you have chosen wisely in your purchase.

This book, first and foremost, is a guide to improving your memory. It will enable you to become more successful, whether you are in college or just generally, in all endeavors which might benefit from the memorization, understanding, and categorization of terminology and concepts.

I have attempted to put forth in writing, in a concise and informative manner, without any presumptions about the intelligence of the reader, a series of memory techniques which are believed to be capable of aiding the learner in all things requiring memorization as well as both sequential and non-sequential recollection. Furthermore, dear reader, I want to inform you that there will be no "dumbing down" of the content of this book. I respect you and I will not dishonor your intelligence by doing so. I think that the mere fact that you have picked up this book at all is, in a way, proof of your curiosity, which is essential to most learning, and your desire to improve yourself. So, as the author of this book, I formally welcome you to the age-old discipline of the Art of Memory, and I deeply hope that you may benefit from its contents.

As for the work itself, it is broken up into thirty two parts. In the first few parts, we discuss the origins and nature of memory and how they relate to human survival. In the intermediary parts of the book, we discuss several techniques of the Art of Memory. And, in the final parts, a series of visualization techniques are given that should be used in combination with the intermediary parts' contents.

Furthermore, this book introduces for the first time to the study of Mnemotechnics a foundational, scientific nomenclature. It is my desire that this new lexicon of terms will enable more efficient communication between practitioners of this art for the sake of its development, and to help bring the Art of Memory into the scientific mainstream.

Sincerely,
M.A. Kohain

Part 1 | What is the Purpose of Memory?

"Your most noble nature's shining instance, your mind's most vital loftiness, your fully formed humanity's kindness, illustrious Lord Heinz, have summoned, compelled and driven me to reveal to you, as a personal monument of that respect with which I embrace you, one child from among the principal children of my genius, conceived and formed a long time ago. Its main theme is the composition of images, signs and ideas, for the purpose of mastering universal invention, arrangement and memory." – Giordano Bruno the Nolan(1)

The quote above has been placed at the start of this book for the reason that it completely encapsulates the author's personal motivations, for I see you, the reader, as the one whom I serve in writing this book, its purpose being to share with you the science of the development of memory and its artificial arrangement. So, to begin on this journey, I first ask you this question: Why, at all, do we form memories in the first place?

If, when a primate finds itself being hunted by some tiger, is it beneficial for that primate to *know* that such an animal is in fact a predator? Indeed, it seems that the appearance, the regular quantity, the abilities, the size, strength, and whereabouts of a predator need be remembered by a preyed-upon-animal so that it may flee or avoid danger when a predator is sighted. Such is perhaps the evolutionary origin of memory in human beings, although in modern times the predator is not a tiger but rather a biology exam, a speech or a math test – success or failure in relation to those now determines one's fate.

What does the college student worry about and fear the most? Is it the wild, hungry, carnivorous pack of lions chasing him or her about the dormitory? Or is it simply failure regarding the dreaded midterm and essay? For just as knowledge of the existence of the various predators of the jungle is necessary for survival in that environment, so too is the knowledge of the content of an exam in the modern classroom. Therefore, would it not be beneficial to our happiness and survival in this day and age to improve our memories and our speed of memorization, so that we may conquer and overcome these modern obstacles to survival? This should probably be considered as a necessary adaptation for many of us, certainly for anyone that finds themselves confronted with a challenging professor.

If you are reading this book, I believe you must truly be a studious person because the desire to succeed is, while natural, rarely acted upon intelligently. Nowadays, survival is more than ever dependent upon one's ability to learn, that is, to memorize, recall, and effectively apply vast quantities of invented knowledge in a diverse array of environments, as opposed to merely relying upon instinct. By and large, success seems to be impossible without first *learning* and *knowing* one's surroundings, which, in this modern era, are informatically extensive relative to the environment of our evolutionary becoming.

But how *exactly* does memory relate to survival? Rather, which specific types of memory contribute toward man's survival in his ancient environment? First and foremost, and certainly applicable to many other species of animal, are the memories of past feeding grounds; that is, areas where nutrients were or are present, seasonally or otherwise. Furthermore, locations where predators are known to hunt and live must also be remembered and subsequently avoided. In other words, he must remember where to find food and where to avoid so as not to become food.

Secondly, the appearances of edible foods and predators, among many other things, must be remembered. In our modern society, for example, it is important to remember who to trust and even how a trustworthy person will behave! It seems that the rules of the jungle have not changed, only the appearance of the jungle has.

Thirdly, it is necessary to remember the meanings implied by certain behaviors as well as how to perform them. These behaviors will probably have something to do with either avoiding predators or finding food. For example, the chimpanzee is known to use sticks to gather termites for consumption. If the chimpanzee did not remember how to perform this action, how could he eat termites? Also, how could a monkey survive if it could not remember that trees can be safe zones from predators? Memory is therefore, and obviously so, very crucial to the survival of preyed-upon animals.

Fourthly, the animal must remember how abundant in resources certain areas are relative to one another and choose accordingly for the sake of its migrations.

And lastly, I think the animal must remember those areas of which he has already been and which no longer, for the time being at least, have the resources by means of which he may continue to survive. Likewise for modern man, each of these functions of memory enable him to confront the various obstacles to his survival.

Part 2 | How are Memories Formed?

In the previous section we went into cursory detail about the origins of memory; the memories causal relationship with survival, but now we ask the question: How are lasting memories formed in the first place?(2) Or, what exactly needs to occur for a memory to become "long-term?"

First, I am going to ask you to imagine something very strange: Albert Einstein riding a pink, tasseled bicycle down the street while playing the saxophone and wearing googly-eyed glasses. Now, if you saw this in real life, how would you react? Without doubt, you would be surprised. You would probably feel that this sight is very out of the ordinary, strange, and not something commonly seen. For starters, a grown man probably would not ride a pink bicycle in public, let alone a very famous and very dead physicist. Nor would any sane person attempt to play the saxophone at the same time as riding a bike, out of fear of crashing; to punctuate this strangeness, I don't believe it is often that we see a man wear googly-eyed glasses in public except on Halloween, and certainly not in combination with the aforementioned. Altogether this is a very extraordinary and unbelievable sight that would probably leave a lasting impression [or memory] upon you if you saw it in public. Thus, perhaps, we can say that, in part, the trick to improving our ability to create long-term memories depends on the fact that amazing and or ludicrously strange images are more easily remembered than ones which are common, possible, and boring. Therefore, if we want to memorize some terminology for our next exam, should we not then attempt to somehow make that terminology strange? This, in part, is the *art of memory*; that is, to add strangeness to the dull and variability to the repetitive. It is like the great Cicero says: *"Now nature herself teaches us what we should do. When we see in everyday life things that are petty, ordinary, banal, we generally fail to remember them, because the mind is not being stirred by anything novel or marvelous. But if we see or hear something exceptionally base, dishonorable, extraordinary, great, unbelievable, or laughable, that we are likely to remember a long time... Thus nature shows that she is not aroused by the common, ordinary event, but is moved by new or striking occurrences."*

For example, if I should ask you to remember a long string of numbers, say fifty random numbers in ten minutes, will this be an easy task for you to complete in such a short amount of time? Likely not. And why is this? Why is it so difficult to quickly memorize and recall long strings of numbers? Is it perhaps because the individual numbers are not "marvelous" enough? Then, if by adding strangeness to these numbers, do you think that we may be able to memorize them more rapidly than normal?

What is it exactly that a string of numbers may lack or have in relation to its affinity for memory? I think the answer is variability, but sameness too can be useful. Variability is important, for each of those fifty is a number and have no striking appearances in themselves, and such is not conducive to memory. However, we must say that not merely is variability important but also sameness in some circumstances. For example, at first glance, the number 1,111,111 shall likely be more easily remembered then the number 1,427,385. And why is this? I think it is because the number 1,111,111 requires only two datums to be remembered, whereas the number 1,427,385 requires 13. How is it that one has two and the other thirteen? I will show you: In the number 1,111,111, we must merely remember that the number only contains ones and that there are seven of them. But in the number 1,427,385, we must first remember the seven different numbers of the sequence and secondly their specific order, which regards six pieces of information (1 then 4, 4 then 2, etc).

Now, I ask you, what is seemingly the most powerful human sense? You will probably say the sense of sight. The famous Chinese proverb "A picture is worth a thousand words" definitely holds true, and that is because what is seen, more often than not, has more impact upon the mind then the other senses. Would you rather be blind or deaf? I think most would choose the sense of sound to give up. And why is that? Is it perhaps because the sense of sight is basically the greatest, most powerful, and most useful sense of all? So also in the act of memorization, I think it is most prudent to focus on the application of imagery to those things we wish to memorize. Thusly, the Art of Memory is greatly visual, for we remember that which is most profound and apparent to our senses, and our sense of sight being our greatest sense, therefore, is capable of receiving the greatest impressions. This is why, of course, a professor that uses visual demonstration to show a concept exceeds another professor when the other merely demonstrates by writing. For one shows the real nature of the concept, i.e., its substance, activity, form, and, or, appearance, and the other only its spoken form which most of the time, in English, says nothing about the actual nature of the thing in itself.

Part 3 | The Art of Memory

The Art of Memory, simply put, is an art form that seeks to improve upon man's natural ability to memorize and recall; and that which is produced above and beyond man's natural memory, by means of the Art of Memory, is called the Artificial Memory. If you have ever found yourself faced with a daunting midterm or the general prospect of needing to memorize hundreds of new terms and definitions, the Art of Memory can push your ability to memorize that information beyond your natural capability to do so. It is simply a faster and more efficient method for taking information from one place, a book for example, and placing it in another place, your brain.

Does the Art of Memory sound complicated to you? Well, you are in luck, for the task of creating this Artificial Memory is diminished by the fact that the most useful techniques of the Art are few in number and even by themselves are extremely useful. Soon it will be clear that it is in fact quite easy to implement the Art of Memory and that it can be used anywhere, anytime, and by anyone that wants to be better at succeeding in any task that requires memorization and recollection.

Have you have ever felt inferior to your classmates when studying for your Physics midterm, for example? Do you feel that you are unable to get As and Bs on your exams, no matter how hard you study your textbook? Are you someone that just wants to learn a new science for no other reason than to become smarter, but you feel the task may be too great? Or perhaps you consider yourself someone like poor old Montaigne: *"There is nobody less suited than I am to start talking about memory. I can hardly find a trace of it in myself. I doubt if there is any other memory in the world as grotesquely faulty as mine is!... I may be a man of fairly wide learning, but I retain nothing."* (3)

Can the Art of Memory help you overcome these obstacles? The short answer is yes, and not only will you succeed in your endeavors, but in comparison to your peers you will likely exceed them greatly. How does the Art of Memory confer such benefits? Well, partly because the average student does not utilize the techniques of this art, for they do not know about them in the first place; therefore, you will have a leg up in comparison to them when it comes time to prepare for your exams. Furthermore, if you are proficient in this art, I guarantee that you will be able to memorize every single one of the concepts and terms for your upcoming tests in a matter of hours, and these will not just be fleeting memories. Instead they will be enduring and easy recallable long term memories.

If you were to ask a group of your peers, "How many of you have used mnemonic devices to memorize a series of textbook terms or an outline to a speech?" I bet very few of them would even know what a mnemonic device is, let alone have used one in practice. To me this is very disconcerting, since not being able to remember something when you need to can result in very drastic, negative consequences.

Let me ask you another question to help lead us into the upcoming parts of the book: Where is memory? To answer this question, I say that the memory, of course, exists in the mind, and therefore in substance the memory necessarily *is* mind. For, as Aristotle says: *"Memory is, therefore, neither Perception nor Conception, but a state of affection of one of these, conditioned by a lapse of time… there is no such thing as memory of the present while present, for the present is object only of perception, and the future of expectation, but the object of memory is the past. All memory, therefore, implies a time elapsed; consequently only those animals which perceive time remember, and the organ whereby they perceive time is also that whereby they remember."*(4)

Thus, the Art of Memory is an art form which has as its object of affection the very human mind itself. Then, how could we call ourselves diligent students of mind, or users of mind, without first being knowledgeable of the techniques of the Art which has been developed solely for the improvement of the a very important part of the soul of the human being?

Now, like almost every human art, whether it is painting, fixing cars, blacksmithing, computer programming, or sports, etc., there are associated tools and objects upon which those tools are used. So then, what are the tools of the Art of Memory and upon what do they act? Just as one might say that you cannot be a blacksmith without an anvil or the right hammer, or that you can't play football without an actual football and some sort of field, neither can you conduct memory successfully without its associated devices and a functioning human mind itself.

Therefore, let's define the Art of Memory as the application of mnemonic devices upon the space of the human mind for the ultimate goal of improving human memory and recall, whereby the success of the art is determined by one's ability to use these tools.

Part 4 | Mnemonic Devices

What is a mnemonic device? In analogy we should probably think of it as the combination of a paintbrush and the techniques associated with its use. Continuing with the analogy, the canvas, of course, is the mind itself and the paints are our experiences. Now, sure we could use our hands to smear the paint on, and one might even become fairly good at that, but would the quality of such finger painting ever remotely approach that of a da Vinci or Rembrandt? In my humble opinion, that would be practically impossible. According to the Art of Memory the vibrancy, style, and detail of your memories will improve well beyond what you would normally be capable of producing with your natural faculties.

Furthermore, mnemonic devices are not just ordinary human inventions, for they are entirely immaterial and yet retain the property of locality. So, where are they located? The truth is, as was said to before, that they exist within the mind of the practitioner as parts of the practitioner's very psyche, and are extremely personal for partly this reason.

Are mnemonic devices distinct from the mind like a hammer is distinct from the hand? The answer to that is probably a resounding no, for when using the Art of Memory your mnemonic devices become the very foundations of your mind as they are necessarily composed from the matter and energies of your own brain and awareness. Then again perhaps, in another way, they are like the hammer, for the spirit may be said to roam and animate the city of the mind, seemingly disassociated from its substance.

Within the mind, what form do these mnemonic devices take when they represent the information desired to be remembered? Mostly, as was stated before, they are visual. However, their forms are actually multiple in the sense that objects which can be seen can also have attributed to them potentially non-visual properties. For example, something can be seen to have a smooth surface or to appear dirty and smelly, but these are more distinctly known, or understood, through the senses of touch and smell. So the point is, that while mnemonic devices are basically visual, in detail they can have multiple types of sensory data attributed to them. Further, you will find that a sort of artificial synesthesia may form within your mind, by means of the use of these mnemonic devices, as you begin to see textures, to see smells, to visualize sounds, etc.

Now quantitatively speaking, 'mnemonic devices' is a universal category such that the singular instances of the applications of mnemonic devices are infinite in number yet generally labeled. These singular instances of the application of mnemonic devices are termed as *Mnemonic Units* (MUs). An MU is defined as a single instance of the use of a particular mnemonic device.

Just as a single brushstroke of a paintbrush is just that, each MU represents a single datum of experiential information that has been symbolized by means of mnemotechnics. For example, maybe we desire to use the image of an *apple* to represent the letter "A." This apple is a single MU.

Is the MU itself dividable? Yes. For example, our symbol 'apple' has a shape, color, and quantity, etc., naturally attributed to it in appearance, and all of these combined form the single image of an 'apple.' This image-apple should be thought of as a singular entity, just like you would think an atom to be when considering it as part of a molecule, but which in itself is formed from even smaller particles. Subsequently, let us define a new term, the *Mnemonic Unit Component* (MUC), which for our apple may be its shape, color, or quantity, etc, and which the image of an apple itself might be for an even greater MU, such as one composed of the images for those letters chosen to represent some word that also contains the letter A.

Therefore, in any particular application of some type of mnemonic device, an MU may possibly have a great number of these MUCs applied to it, which are totally modifiable as is necessary for the combining or creation of symbols. Perhaps, for example, you want to color the apple black to symbolize something totally unrelated to whatever the MU for the letter A is being used to help symbolize. This, then, would be a modification of the apple's MUC for color. MUC modifications are very helpful when the need for categorizing large numbers of MUs becomes necessary. In other words, a MUC is a type of 'operator' which acts upon some component of the nature of a particular MU in order to signify some particular property of the thing to be memorized. Again, for example, we might modify some component of an MU for the element Hydrogen in order to denote that it is a Diatomic Non-metal.

In the next chapter we will discuss the Thirty-Two Methods for symbol generation, that is, MU generation.

Key Terms:

Mnemonic Unit (MU): *A single instance of the application of a mnemonic device, a symbol. As for example, an apple when it symbolizes the letter 'A.'*

Mnemonic Unit Component (MUC): *A component of an MU. An MUC can also show secondary symbolism, referencing or sharing a property of another MU.*

Part 5 | Thirty Two Methods for Acquiring Images to Represent Words

The Thirty Two Methods for image generation consists of thirty two distinct ways of deriving imagery to symbolize the various words or things that we need to remember. This is the first time since the days of Giordano Bruno that such a list has been presented. Contained within this list is a practically exhaustive number of means to create symbols. The authors own source for a multitude of these is a famous work authored by Giordano Bruno titled *On the Composition of Images, Signs & Ideas*, published in 1591. If there is ever a time when you are unable to naturally derive an image, these Thirty Two will doubtless aid you in accomplishing the task. The Thirty Two Methods are as follows:

Self-reference | This method is the simplest. It is also very effective. For example, if you want to memorize a word like "dog" or "house" then all you need to do is recall the image of a "dog" or "house."

Nature | This method can be very generally applied. It works by finding some natural symmetry between the word or idea that you want to recall and the image used for recollection. For example, I would remember the word "milk" by the image of some object that is colored white. Similarly, I might recall the word "farm" by the image of a sheep.

Syllables and Letters | When dealing with more complex topics and terminologically dense subject matter, we can use the phonetic method for memorizing words. This technique is probably the most reliable and universally applicable and therefore the most valuable of all the methods for generating imagery given in this part. It is a "brute force" technique and will work for any word formed from a combination of English letters and can even be applied for memorizing foreign languages.

We say that it is the most universally applicable because most words are not visually self-referential. In it, we apply the Two Alphabets technique to the formation of images for the various words and things that we want to remember. This technique is further described in the following two chapters wherein two lists of images, representing the (1) twenty six letters of the English alphabet and (2) the most common syllables in the English language, are given. The images from those lists can then be further combined when the need arises to symbolize three or more letters.

Shape | This technique is one that you will probably very rarely use, for English words and letters are not themselves visually impactful to memory. This technique aims to create images based off of the shapes of the words or letters to be memorized. For example, for the letter "O" we might envision a hole.

Or for the letter 'I' we might envision a Greek column.

Uniqueness | According to some unique property, distinguishing feature, or mark of the thing to be remembered, we derive suitable imagery. For example, we may remind ourselves of a snake from a sinusoidal track; a Ram by referencing its horns with spiral curvature; a crab by its shell; twins through equality; a lion by a mane; In fact, this is the way in which the astrologers of old preserved in memory the characters of the signs of Zodiac.

Gesture | Gesture can be very implicative of certain states of mind. If, for example, we are desirous of remembering the word love, we may imagine the image of two figures embracing each other, and hatred by the opposite, by figures turned away, separated and disconnected.

Custom or Institution without Reason, Etymology or Nature | Some things are merely signified a certain way out of custom, without reason, or without reference to the nature of the object signified.

Convention or Historical Precedent | From convention or historical precedent we form images to represent things based upon the past relevance of the thing signifying to the thing signified. *"For example, we signify peace with an olive tree, not because the power or significance of peace is in the olive tree per se, but because it recalls to mind the story in which Neptune gave the horse as a gift to the Athenians to use in war, the horse sprang out of the* *earth when Neptune's trident struck it, and Athena presented the Athenians with the olive tree after his spear had shaken the ground. The olive evolved into an archetype of peace, at least on the grounds that it was distinct in purpose from the sign of war the horse."*

Temporal Symmetry | MUs may be derived based upon some concordant temporal existence with the thing to be remembered, that is to say, according to either fortune or nature. For example, a human life is symbolic of a great many different phenomena, for *"all things enjoy helpless infancy, a growing period, maturity, decline, and death."*

Analogy | *"By analogy it has been reasoned that from the motion of lower things as well as from the effects of higher and invisible things and from the motion of higher things as well as from the causes of lower things, we receive the impulse to signify. From sensible substances, I say, there arises the intelligible, that which can be understood."* Images may be formed through analogy with the things to be remembered.

The Concrete from the Abstract and Vice Versa | From the concrete comes the abstract, for example from white we may recall whiteness and vice versa.

Correlation | *"From the relative comes the correlative, just as, for example, from the adjacent master we conclude the existence of a servant. We can depict a giant on a small pebble by virtue of relation and comparison, while a man is proportioned to the size of a single fly, and many people standing together to a swarm of many ants."*

Same Effect from the Same or Similar Cause | We derive images for the things to be remembered based upon their having similar causes.

Same Antecedents | *"From the antecedents we divine the cause, as, for example, from clouds rising up in the south and from hens rolling in the dust we presage rain."*

Concomitants | *"From concomitants we divine the cause, as, for example, when we see fire kindled from flame."*

Consequence | *"From consequences we divine the cause, as, for example, we understand that it has rained when the ground is damp."*

From Results We Derive the Reason | *"From results we divine the reason."* For example, from the image of some book we may recall its author, or from the presence of flies, a corpse.

The Divided from the Unified | From something composed sensibly arises a division [divisum] which is not sensible, as, for example, from "alive" [animalis] comes "soul, life force" [anima].

The Unified from the Components and Vice Versa | From the images of something's components we may derive that which is produced from their combination as, for example, we might recall the word beer from the image of barley and a barrel and vice versa.

From the Conjunct Arises the Adjunct | For example, we may symbolize a sick person by the image of a bed they will lie in and a doctor beside it.

From the Tool We Derive the Skill | *"For example, the astrologer by the astrolabe or the farmer by his hoe or his plow"*

Historical Action | *"The agent [agens] is recognized by his mode of action [actio], or the receiver of action [patiens] by reason of his suffering his receptivity [passio]. For example, a corpse dragged by the wheels behind a particular leader's chariot leads us to recall Hector, and someone slicing through a complicated knot with a sword reminds us of Alexander, who thus swiftly untied the Gordian knot."*

Location from Object | *"For example, from [a] Roman, Rome, from [an] Italian, Italy; and the reverse: from the place, the object located there, as, for example, from treasure chest, treasure, from the wine jar, wine, since wine does not exist by itself."*

Appropriate Action | *"Likewise, from sensible activity we understand the imperceptible, as, for example, from adulterer with adulteress we understand adultery, from someone murdering somebody, murder."*

From the Part, the Whole | *"For example, from the wheel, the chariot, from four or five people together we understand people."*

From the Whole, the Part | *"For example, from a blind man we understand weakness of the eyes."*

From the Proportional the Jointly Proportional | *"For example, from the potter who diligently handles and spins his wheel we understand divine judgment and predestination."*

Property from Object | From one image having some property of something we derive said property. For example, from the image of a "strong man" we derive "strength."

Cause and Effect | *"From the effect we infer the cause, and from the cause the effect; for example, from something skillfully made we understand skill; from an architect architecture, and the reverse."*

Allusion | *"Likewise, from a certain allusion we intuit that to which allusion is made. For example, from a little old woman standing between two very young and pretty girls we comprehend an eclipse, the earth's position between Sun and Moon."*

Contrariety | We are very much inclined to remember opposites. For example, to remember someone that is very wise we might imagine the image of a very foolish person.

Rhyme | For example, from the word "why," we can imagine a fly, someone or something flying, or anything that rhymes with the word "fly."

Part 6 | The First Alphabet

The first of the phonetic devices is called *The First Alphabet*. It is called this because in it we associate with every letter of the English alphabet various images. These images we will use to help form our MUs and MUCs. In using this technique, it is necessary to pay great attention to which images are chosen and which letters from the to-be-memorized word will partake in the formation of the MU. This is because the MUs themselves, even though they are reduced in complexity compared to the original word, are still capable of becoming too regular in appearance and therefore more difficult to bind into memory. One must take great care to insure that all images are as variable as possible.

The First Alphabet:

C	Humanoids	Substances	Objects	Qualities	Actions and Affections (add "ing" and/or "ed")	Locations
A	Admiral	Alligator	Apple	Amber	Agony/Art	Alley
B	Belly Dancer	Bear	Brick/Bottle/Bread	Blue	Bash/Bake	Boat/Bedroom
C	Chemist/Caesar	Cat	Chair/Cushion	Cash	Choke/Churn	Church/Car/Cave/Carriage
D	Doctor/Detective	Dove/Dog	Door	Dust	Dead/Drip	Doorway/Desert
E	Executive	Elephant	Emerald	Emerald	Eat	Embers
F	Farmer	Fish	Fire	Foam	Fish	Fence/Fortress/Feast
G	Gorilla	Gorilla	Gear/Gift	Gold	Glue/Grip	Gass
H	Hockey Player	Hippo	Helmet	Hair	Hang	Hole/Hill
I	Infantryman	Iguana	Instrument (Musical)/Eye	Ice	Ignite	Igloo
J	Judge	Jaguar	Junk	Jewels	Jab/Jump	Courtroom
K	King	Kangaroo/Killer whale	Kite	Kelp	Kick/Kiss	Throne room
L	Librarian	Lion	Leafs/Light bulb	Light	Lash/Lunge	Library/Log Cabin
M	Maid	Monkey	Mirror	Mud	Mangle/Mold/Moan	Mountain/Mill/Mansion
N	Naked Woman	Neanderthal	Knife/Nest/Nail	Net	Nail	Crucifix
O	Old Man	Owl	Oar	Orange	Oil/Open	Ocean/Oasis
P	Priest	Penguin	Pants	Purple	Punch/Pat	Prison/Boxing Ring
Q	Queen	Squid	Quilt	Quilted	Squash/Stab	Squash Court
R	Ronin	Rhino	Rake	Red	Roast	Roof/Railway/R. Car
S	Singer/Slave/Sailor	Snake	Shovel	Silver	Sliced	Stage
T	Tailor	Tiger	Tree/Tie/Telephone	Titanium	Tickle/Tie	Temple
U	Usher/Yourself	Smurf	Utensil/Umbrella	Ugly	Bump/Buck	Ceiling
V	Vagrant	Vulture	Vine	Velvet	Veil	Vineyard
W	Wise Man	Walrus	Wine	Wax	Wash	Watchtower
X	Mathematician	Fox	Shield	Crosses	Mix	Cross street
Y	Yodeler	Yak	Martini Glass/Fork	Yellow	Yank	Forked Road
Z	Zoo Keeper/Czar	Zebra	Laser	Z. Stripes	Zap	The Clouds
	Humanoids	Non-humanoids	Objects			

It is entirely acceptable for you to add your own images to this table and this is in fact encouraged, for as Cicero says: "*…why do we wish to rob anybody of his initiative, so that, to save him from making any search himself, we deliver to him everything searched out and ready? Then again, one person is more struck by one likeness, and another more by another.*"(5)

You will probably notice a significant pattern in the images for each letter, which is that the word for each image starts, in most cases, with the letter of the alphabet associated with it in the table. This is so that in observing the image we may naturally recall the associated letter of the word desired to be remembered. Putting it another way, would it make sense or at all be simple to recall a letter which has no similitude with the image? Therefore, the desired term to be remembered and the letter sequence implied by the image-symbol, the MU, have the same sounding first letter based upon the table. However, it needs to be mentioned that we do not need to have the same first letter for our image, but only necessarily something which would reasonably enable us to recall the first letter, or first sound, of the word to be remembered.

Now follows is an example of this technique. In this example we create a series of MUs to represent the major components of all *Eukaryotic cells* and finally bind them all together into an even greater MU.

EXAMPLE: What are the main components of a Eukaryotic cell? For our purposes, these are the *Nucleus, Mitochondria, Golgi Apparatus, Endoplasmic Reticulum* and *Smooth Endoplasmic Reticulum, Lysosomes, Plasma Membrane, DNA,* and *Cytosol*. Now there are definitely more components to Eukaryotic cells, but those here listed are, for the most part, the largest in size and most widely known. We will not speak of their definitions or specific functions here, but MUs for such definitions and descriptions of functions may be likewise created and linked.

Our first term and most general term is "Eukaryotic Cell," which when converted to an MU will serve as the foundation for the rest, a kind of *nexus* for the potentially subordinate images. For the term "Eukaryotic Cell," which images shall we apply from the First Alphabet? Let us break down the word into some intelligently chosen phonetic components. Normally we would approach this break-down by choosing an image associated with the letter E, but because of the sound of the word, "yoo-kae-ree-ah-tihk," wherein the sound "yoo" (Eu) has the same sound as the letter *u* as it is spoken when reciting the alphabet, it would be more appropriate to choose an image associated with that letter.(6) Thus, we choose the image *Usher*. This usher will serve as the first image in your nexus for the subsequent association of the other MUs.

The other letters that we choose should represent the other most prominent sounds of the word to be broken down; which sounds are most prominent may differ from person to person, and your ability to find them will improve the more you use the technique, but for this example we will choose the letters *k* and *r*. Thus, phonetically, we have the sound "*yoo-kae-ree*," which should have enough similarity to the original word-to-be-memorized to force its recollection through the observation and understanding of the

MU. Our image for the letter *k* is a *Throne Chair* and our image for the letter *r* is a *Wreath*.

So, we have for our first MUCs:

Yoo/U(Eu) – USHER
Kae/K – THRONE CHAIR
Ahr/Ree/R – WREATH

Next, bring these images together to form our first combined MU. Subsequently, let us envision the image of an usher sitting on a throne chair with a wreath around his neck and fix it within memory. This process will be expanded upon in the following chapter with the introduction of the Second Alphabet. Applying the Second Alphabet will greatly speed up and improve the process of MU formation using the Phonetic Method.

Not only will this combined image serve well to help us recall the term "Eukaryote," the very effort put into the creation of the MU, the searching and finding of the appropriate images and their association will help transform the MU into a long-term memory. The following images for the remaining terms should then be bound in some way to our *Mnemonic Unit Nexus* (MUN). The next terms to be remembered and their associated MUs:

Nucleus – N,C,L – *A naked woman, holding cash and covering her privates with leaves*

Mitochondria –M,I,C – *A monkey, frozen in ice, being choked.*

Golgi Apparatus – G,O, A,P – *A little girl with an owl on her right arm, and apple in her left hand, and being patted on the head.*

Endoplasmic Reticulum – E,D,P,L, R,T,C,U – *An Executive, holding a dog, and, wearing no pants, with lash marks on his legs. He is riding a Rhino made of titanium that is standing on a pile of cash and is holding an umbrella for the executives.*

Smooth Endoplasmic Reticulum, S,M,E,D,P,R,T,C,U – *A muddy shovel in the hand of an identical EDPL as shown in the previous image, also riding on the rhino. Thus, on the Rhino, there are seated two EDPLs.*
Lysosomes – L,I,S,O – *A lion, playing a silver guitar, opening a door.*
Plasma Membrane – P,L,M,B – *A priest holding a light bulb in his right hand and a mirror in his left while standing on a pile of bricks.*
DNA –D,N,A – *A dinosaur*
Cytosol – S,I,T,O – *A snake, wearing a tie, with its back end wrapped around a flute and with an orange in its mouth.*

Now that we have formed our individual MUs we may further combine them to create a multiform image for the recollection of these various cellular structures: First, imagine the *usher* sitting on a *throne chair* with a *wreath* around his neck. Next, let's have him *choking* a *monkey* that is frozen in *ice* to his left, and have him using his other hand to *pat* a *little girl on the head* who has an *owl* perched on her right arm and an *apple* in her left hand. Behind the usher, place the *two executives* riding a *titanium rhino* that is standing in a *doorway*. And next to them, place the *lion* with the *silver guitar, opening* the door to let them through. In front of the usher, lying promiscuously on the ground, observe the *naked woman* holding *cas*h and covering her privates with *leaves*. Further, let's have the woman playing the *flute* with the *tie-wearing snake* wrapped around it and with an *orange* in its mouth. Then place the *priest* to the right of the woman and make him staring at her in disdain. Lastly, imagine a *dinosaur* to the left of the woman, biting her leg.

I tell you, you will not forget this combined image, for it is ludicrous and perhaps even offensive, yet such imagery is amazingly conducive to rapid memorization. As a general rule, Cicero likewise states that: *"We ought, then, to set up images of a kind that can adhere longest in the memory. And we shall do so if we establish likenesses as striking as possible; if we set up images that are not many or vague, but doing something; if we assign to them exceptional beauty or singular ugliness; if we dress some of them with crowns or purple cloaks, for example, so that the likeness may be more distinct to us; or if we somehow disfigure them, as by introducing one stained with blood or soiled with mud or smeared with red paint, so that its form is more striking, or by assigning certain comic effects to our images, for that, too, will ensure our remembering them more readily."*(7) Furthermore, as you may have realized, this is also partly why we say that mnemonic devices are very personal – that they need to sometimes stay personal because of their strange imagery.

Part 7 | The Second Alphabet

The "Second Alphabet" is used in the same manner as the first but is entirely syllabic. It should be used in conjunction with the first alphabet when it is deemed reasonable by the practitioner, but neither should be considered as primary relative to the other. Instead, they should be considered as equal in power but, generally speaking, the syllabic is more specific, since syllables naturally imply more than one sound and therefore imply more information about the term to be remembered. Furthermore, the images in the following alphabet may be drawn forth from the table and combined in the same manner as was shown using the First Alphabet for the creation of MUs for the various major Eukaryotic cellular components. It is suggested that both alphabets be used in concert.

This syllable-based mnemonic alphabet is composed of the most common and most mnemonically practical first, second, and third syllables:

Syllables	Images
AB	Abbot/Abs/Abby/Abyss/Abused
AC	Ace/Acid/Acne/Actor/Academy
AD	Ad/Black Adder/Addict
AG	Agora/Agate/Agreement
AI	Air/Aim/First Aid/Aisle/Aikido/Airport/Airplane/Airbrush
AK	Akimbo/Akvavit/AK-47
AL	Alarm/Allergy/Aluminum Bat/Almond/Altar/Alien
AM	Amoeba/Amigo/Amen/Amputee/Ambulance/Anabolic Steroid
AN	Anaconda/Ants/Anchor/Anchovy/Angel/Angle
AP	Apc/App/Apples/Apostle/Apocrypha
AR	Ark/Arm/Armor/Aroma/Arsenal/Archer/Art/Arbalist/Arachnid/Armadillo/Arrow
AS	Ash/Asthma/Astronomy/Asexual/Ascension/Asphalt/Assassin
AT	Atom/Atrophy/Attic/Attila
AU	Aunt/Aura/Auger/Aurora/Automobile
AV	Avenue/Aviator/Aviatrix/Avalanche
AW	Awe/Awning/Awakes/Award
AY	Ayatollah/Ayurveda
BA	Bat/Bar/Basketball/Bath/Bathtub/Baby/Bank/Barn/Baal/Ball/Badger/Batman/Barley/Baboon/Bamboo/Bartender
BE	Bed/Beg/Bee/Beans/Belly/Besiege/Beatle/Berserker
BI	Bile/Bible/Bite/Biochip/Billion/Bird/Birdcage/Birdhouse/Billiards/Bicycle/Bicycle Rider
Bl	Blocks/Blood/Blimp/Blond/Black/Blueberry/Blasphemy/Bloody Mary
BO	Book/Boa Constrictor/Bowl/Bomb/Box/Boxer/Boar/Bouncer
BR	Bra/Brie Cheese/Brown/Branch/Bride/Brain/Brownies/Brail
BU	Bug/Butt/Bull/Burger/Buggy/Burka/Bullet/Bunker/Burial/Butterfly/Butter
CA	Cab/Can/Cards/Carpenter/Calf/Cake/Cage/Cave/Caveman/Cartoon/Cabbage/Carpet/Cardinal
CE	Cedar/Centaur/Celadon (color)/Censored/Cello/C.E.O./Celery/Celestial
CH	Chin/Chip(s)/Indian Chief/Chinese/Chimpanzee/Chicken/Cheerleader
CI	Cigarette/Cigar/Cicero/Circle/Circuit/Circlet/Cithern
CL	Claw/Club/Clay/Clock/Climb/Cloak/Clam/Cliff/Clown/Clover
CO	Cod/Cog/Cow/Comb/Cot/Cone/Coach/Cornet/Comet/Cookie/Copper/Coal/Coffin/Computer
CR	Crab/Crow/Cream/Cricket/Crystal/Crowbar/Crucible/Crib/Crate
DA	Dagger/Dart/Daisy
DE	Devil/Desk/Deck/Deer/Deerskin/Dentist
DI	Dice/Dishes/Diary/Diver/Discus/Diamond
DO	Dot/Dojo/Dock/Donkey/Dough/Donut
DR	Drag/Drill/Drop/Dryer/Dragon/Drums/Drumstick/Drummer

EA	Ear/Earlock/Earring/East/Earphone/Earth
EC	Eclipse/Éclair/Eczema/Echidna/Ectoplasm/
ED	Edge/Editor/Editions/Eddy
EL	Elm Tree/Elk/Elf/Electricity/Elderly/Elbow
EM	Embryo/Emperor/Ethernet Cord
ER	Eris/Eraser/Erupted/Erudite
ES	Escort/Estrogen/Essay/Escargot/Esoteric
FA	Fat/Fax Machine/Fan/Face/Falcon/Fairy/Faust
FE	Fez/Femur/Ferret/Feet
FI	Fin/Fig/Five/Film/Filter/Firefly
FL	Flute/Flannel/Flea/Flip/Flask/Fly (bug)
FO	Fox/Formula/Foam/Fountain
FR	Fried/Frog/Frost/French Fries
GA	Gas/Gag/Galaxy/Gate/Gazelle/Gangster/Gallery/Gauze
GE	Geek/German/Generator/Gestapo
GH	Ghost
GI	Gin/Giant/Ginger/Gypsy
GO	Golf/Gown/Goat/Gopher/Goblin
GR	Grey/Green/Gravy/Greek/Grill/Grove/Grapes/Graph
HA	Hat/Halt/Harem/Hades/Hand/Hanger/Hammock/Haircut/Harpy
HE	Hen/Heat/Herb/Heron/Hero/Heart
HI	Hip/Hive/Hiker/Hippy/Hitman/Hipster/Hinge
HO	Hoe/Horn/Hook/Hookah/Hoop/Hose/
IC	Icing
IM	Imp/Imam
IN	Ink/Inkwell/Inn/Injured/Invitation/Inmate/Indian/India
IR	Iron/Iris/Iran
IS	Islam/Islander/Island/Isosceles Triangle/Isis
IT	Itchy/I.T./Computer
IV	Ivory/Ivy/I.V.
KE	Key/Keg/Kendo/Kernel/Kebab/Kettle/Keyboard/Kennel
LA	Lamp/Law/Lace/Lawyer/Lamas/Laughing/Laundry
LE	Letcher/Leap/Lemon/Leech/Lead/Lemur/Leg/Leek/Leopard
LI	Lip/Limo/Lilac/Light/Liver/Lift/Lick/Liquor/License/Lighter
LO	Log/Lox/Lottery Ticket/Loadstone
LU	Luck/Lumber/Luggage/Lullaby

MA	Map/Mage/Marsh/Mall/Mace/Market/Maggots/Mattress/Mail/Marbles/Mason/Mango/Maze/Mace
ME	Melon/Meat/Medic/Messiah/Mercury/Measuring Tape
MI	Microphone/Milk/Missile/Mitten/Minivan/Midget
MO	Mosquito/Mouse/Mole/Moss/Moth/Mop/Mohawk/Moon/Mozart/Moses
MU	Mug/Musket/Musketeer/Muzzle
NA	Napkin/Narwhal/Nachos/Nape
NE	Neck/Newt/Nerd (Scholar)/Nectar/Nebula/Necklace
NI	Nickel/Nike/Nine/Nitro/Ninja/Nipple
NO	Nose/Noel/Knob
NY	Nymph
OA	Oak Tree/Oats
OB	Obelisk/Oba/Obsidian
OC	Occult/Octopus/Ocarina
OD	Odor/Odin/Odyssey/Odalisk
OI	Oil
OL	Olive/Olympics
OM	Omen/Omelet
ON	One/Onyx/Onion/Onager (weapon)/Oneself
OP	Opal/Opium/Optometrist/Opera Singer
OR	Orb/Orc/Orca/Oneiroi/Oracle/Orchid/Organon/Organ (instrument)
OT	Otter/Ottoman
OV	Oval/Oven/Ovary
PA	Pan/Paw/Page/Court Page/Pajamas/Pancake/Passport
PE	Pea/Pen/Pear/Peel/Peek/Penny/Perfume/Pericles/Pearl/Peach
PI	Pi/Pie/Pin/Pig/Pill/Pike/Pipe/Pinky/Pinata/Pitcher/Piano/Pillow/Picnic/Pinball Machine/Pistachios/Pine Tree/Pilot/Pickle
PL	Plywood/Platinum/Plane/Plums/Plumber/Planet/Placenta
PO	Pole/Pot/Police/Portal/Poppy Flower/Potato
PR	Professor/Prism/Prisoner/Protester/Prayer/Prophet/Propane/Pretzel
PU	Pub/Puppy/Putter/Pumpkin/Pump/Punt/Puppet
QU	Quilt/Quail/Quill/Quartz/Quarter
RA	Rat/Rain/Railing/Ramp/Rattle/Rattlesnake/Rabbit/Raven
RE	T-Rex/Referee/Redneck
RI	Rib/Rifle/Ripple/River
RO	Rose/Rod/Roll/Rock/Roman/Roach/Rooster/Rocket/Road/Rosary
RU	Rum/Ruler/Rubber/Rugby/Rudder

SA	Sap/Saw/Sand/Salt/Salon/Saliva/Sacrifice/Sacrum/Safe/Sardine/Sake/Sail
SC	Scar/Scab/Scale/School/Scarf/Scallion/Scoopula/Salmon/Scientist/Scorpion
SE	Sea/Seal/Sew/Seed/Car seat/Settler/Seafood/Seashell/Seahorse
SH	Ship/Shit/Shampoo/Shawl/Shank/Shark/Shower/Shrine/Shylock
SI	Six/Sister/Silk/Sit-up/Sip/Silicon/Siamese Twins/Silo/Siren
SM	Smock/Smoke/Smooth/Blacksmith
SN	Snail/Snort/Snicker/Sniper
SO	Soup/Soil/Sock/Sofa/Soccer Ball/Socket
SP	Spear/Spy/Spit/Speedo/Spinach/Spices/Sphere/Sponge/(Ambrogio) Spinola/Spine/Spacesuit/Space Shuttle/Spider/Spatula
SQ	Squirrel/Square/Squat
ST	Stew/Stab/Steak/Steel/Stream/Stamp/Stadium/Stomach/Star
SU	Sun/Suit/Submarine/Surfboard/Sumo
SY	Sylph/Syringe
TA	Tar/Tan/Tacks/Tape/Tank/Table/Tattoo Artist/Tablespoon/Tambourine
TE	Tea/Ten/Teddy bear/Tetris/Tennis/Teacup
TH	Thug/Throat/Thief/Thread/Thong
TI	Tin/Tick/Time/Tire/Tiptoe/Tic-tac/Ticket/Tissue
TO	Toe/Ton/Tomb/Tome/Tongs/Toxin/Toy/Toddler/Tornado/Toast
TR	Trojan/Tractor/Tripod/Trapeze
TU	Tuba/Tulip/Turbo/Tugboat/Turkey
TW	Twig/(Mark) Twain/Twirl
TY	Typewriter/Tyrant/Typhon
UM	Umpire/Umbilical
UN	United States/Undead
UR	Urn/Uranus/Uranium
VE	Veal/Veil/Vein/Venom/Vegetable/Vertebrae
VI	Videotape/Visor/Virtual/Vizier
WA	Wand/Wall/Walk/Wash/Washer/Warden/Wave/Warlord/Warlock
WE	Web/Wedding/Well/Welder/
WH	Wheel/Wheat/Whip/Whale/Whisky
WI	Wig/Wire/Witch/Wick/Wings/Willow Tree
WO	Wolf/Worm/Wool/Wombat
YO	Yogi/Yogurt/Yoda/Yodel
ZE	Zephyr (Greek Deity)

For any syllables which are not included in this list, please invent your own. Furthermore, notice that there are a great number of syllables in English which are very common because they are present in pronouns, conjunctions, and articles, such as "it" or "yo," so it is also suggested that you create preformed images for all of these (the conjunctions, pronouns, articles, etc) such that when these syllables appear in nouns and verbs, you subsequently know to use entirely different images for them. This will make distinguishing between them in those varying circumstances easier. For example, we might define the conjunction "and" as the image of an anchor and a dog in some visual combination, however multiple unique images for each conjunction should be made in order to avoid any exceptional invariance that might arise when forming MUs for sentences. However, it needs to be mentioned that memorizing information verbatim and allotting imagery specifically to heavily repeated parts of speech like conjunctions is never suggested, but there certainly are circumstances where having imagery for these is helpful, and this will become apparent in Part 18.

As well, images present in the First Alphabet have been excluded from the syllabic alphabet so as to avoid further ambiguity when forming MUs. But for memorizing long strings of numbers it will benefit you to not limit yourself to only the images from the First Alphabet. Instead, you can increase your number of potential images by using the images given in the second alphabet according to their first letters and the numbers those first letters correspond to in the First Alphabet. The numerical equivalencies of the letters in the First Alphabet are shown in a table in Part 15.

You may also appeal to Part 16 for another useful technique regarding this matter.

Now that we have gone over the basic principles of MU formation, we must ask some very important questions: For what reason(s), how, and where should the MUs formed using these two techniques be placed within the mind?

Key Terms:

Mnemonic Unit Nexus (MUN): *The term given to the more general or more universal MU relative to less general MUs, as for example, a MUN might be the MU formed to represent a single chapter heading in a book, a title of some list of things, or, for example, the MU for the term Eukaryotic cell, but only in so far as they are relative to sub-categorical MUs.*

Part 8 | The Method of Loci

The Method of Loci is a very ancient technique and the most essential to the Art of Memory alongside the *Two Alphabets* and the *Thirty Two Method for Image Generation*. It is the mnemonic device which binds MUs formed to a series of ordered locations which have a mostly numerical sequence attributed to them.

Have you ever heard or used the phrase "In the first place?" That expression originally referred to the first location in a series of sequential locations formed according to the Method of Loci as it was used in ancient times. For example, one might have said, *In the first place, there is this or that image*.

But you might ask, why is the concept of location or "space" relevant to memorization and the Art of Memory? Well, simply put, this is because our memories are often naturally bound to locations.

This can easily be seen by the fact that if, for example, you recall your childhood home you will almost always be able to remember the various exceptional happenings associated with that location. If you go deeper into your memories of that location, perhaps to your old bedroom, you may also naturally recall some interesting event that occurred there. You may probably recall the locations of the various furniture, paintings, toys, and books which were placed about your room when you were younger. If you were asked right now, in what part of your room was your bed located in your childhood home, however many years ago, would you be able to answer that question accurately? Probably. And why is that? Is it perhaps because being able to remember particular locations has been extremely important to human beings ever since the days when our survival was predicated upon remembering previous foraging or hunting grounds, or when we needed to remember which areas had predators and therefore needed to be avoided? Probably, we can all agree that in many ways memories about locations were necessary to ancient man's survival, and we take advantage of and adapt this historical location sense to modern learning through the Method of Loci. For why should we not use all of our natural adaptations to excel, instead of letting them become vestigial due to advancements in technology?

To put this point across further, answer this question: If you have ever lost your eye glasses, what is the first thing people might ask you? Probably they would say "where were you when you last had them?" Or they might say to you, "retrace your steps." It is then probably reasonable to suggest that Memory and Locality are neuro-causally intertwined and that the exploitation of our sense of space, as it pertains to memory, would be beneficial and conducive to improvements in our ability memorize spatially significant information, that is, information symbolized in space, i.e., the MU.

Therefore, the Method of Loci is a technique whereby MUs are conditioned to specific locations within a preformed series of locations of either artificial or natural design. By artificial it is meant that the places whereupon the images shall be conditioned are not places which exist in the real world and by natural we mean the opposite, but both are nevertheless localized within the mind. For example, an artificial series of locations might be the throne chamber of a made-up English castle in which there are possibly hundreds if not thousands of different and varying localities within the various wings, halls, and rooms of its area. As for a natural series of locations, your actual home, apartment, or maybe the grocery store you frequent, etc., are also not lacking in potential locations upon which to condition images.

Let us further label our terms to aid in understanding, specification, and explanation: A single location upon which symbolic images (MUs) may be conditioned shall be called a Memory Location (ML). For example, this might be a corner of a room in the mental image of your family house, a table with a lamp on it, a balcony, a steeple, or a window. Basically, anything that stands out. Secondly, a series of MLs existing in a confined zone, such as a single room with multiple corners and objects within it shall be called a Memory Room (MR). Thirdly, let's define a series of these MRs as a Memory Room System (MRS). Any system of these MRSs, for example a series of MRSs or a series of series of MRSs, *ad infinitum*, shall be denoted with exponents after the term, e.g., MRS^2 or MRS^3. Furthermore, anything at the level of MRS^2 or greater will generally be referred to as a *Memory City* or as an mMRS. For example, the made-up castle previously mentioned would be considered an MRS, for it is composed of multiple MRs yet it is in itself potentially compartmental relative to other "distinct buildings and or areas." Likewise all ML, MRs, MRSs, and mMRSs, are each a form of *Memory Field*.

The following diagrams are known as *Mnemographs*. These particular ones are merely examples illustrating the most basic of MRSs. Mnemographs are essentially detailed illustrations showing all hierarchical levels of a memory field. When designing a mnemograph make sure to detail all components of the memory field including the symbolic nature of the MUs attached therein and its entire categorical structure.

*A mnemograph showing the comparison of magnitudes between MLs, MRs, and MRSs

Let us now demonstrate how order and sequence are applied in the Method of Loci to enable memorization of ordered and sequenced data:

Imagine first a square room. Label each corner of the room with the first four letters of the English alphabet, A through D. Now, because of the inherent sequentiality of the letters, we shall know which is first and which is last, which is second and which is third. So if we desired to remember these images in sequence: a *dog*, a *cat*, a *horse*, and a *frog*, we should place them in their respective locations upon our artificial memory locations $A - D$. That is, the dog is placed at A, the cat at B, the horse at C, and the frog at D. This way, because we already have an understanding of the sequence of the rooms, we may infer the sequence of the images because of their placement in those particular locations:

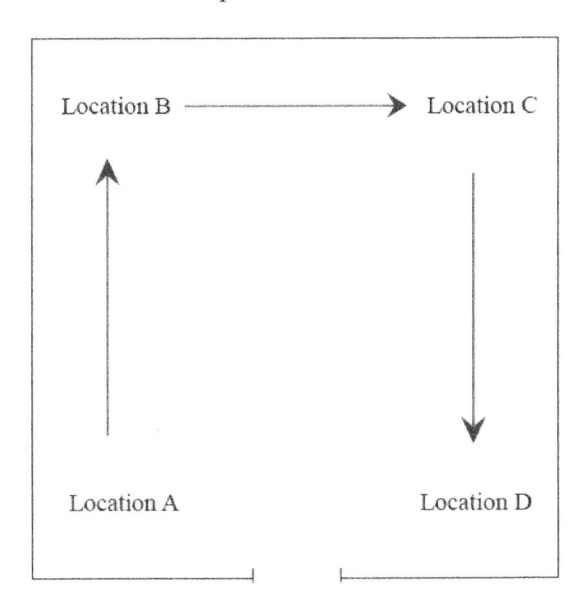

```
Location B ─────────▶ Location C
    ▲                     │
    │                     │
    │                     │
    │                     ▼
Location A            Location D
```

```
        Cat  ─────────▶  Horse
         ▲                 │
         │                 │
         │                 │
         │                 ▼
        Dog               Frog
```

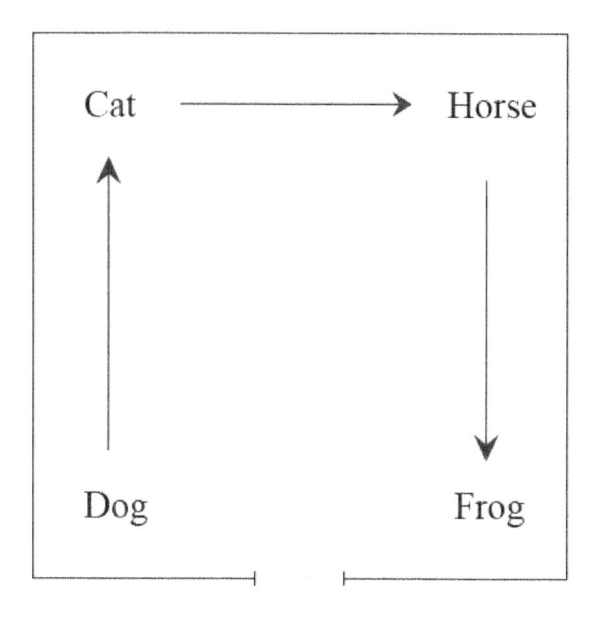

Furthermore, the memory of the relative sequence of these images may be further cultivated by having the MUs causally interact with each other. For example, you may imagine the dog biting the cat's leg, the cat scratching the horses face, and the horse stepping on the frog. This will further increase the mnemonic power of these images in relation to their sequence.

Please note that hypothetically the sequence of several locations may exist *singularly*, that is, within a single MR, across *multiple* MRs, or in some *combination* of these two. Which of the three should be used is determined in part by the type of categorization inherent in the form of the information to be remembered as well as the practitioner's own preference. Similarly, the numeral sequence of MRs, MRSs, and so on may also be determined in this way. This concept can also be applied MUs and their sub-categorical MUCs. The following mnemographs show how this concept is applied to a hypothetical system of MLs, MRs, and MRSs, however these diagrams are not the be-all, and end-all of mnemonic systems. Instead, they should be understood as exemplifying the general principles of sequence and order as they are applied in the Method of Loci.

$$\begin{array}{ccc} 6 & 7 & 8 \\ 5 & 1 & 9 \\ 4 & 3 & 2 \end{array} \quad \begin{array}{ccc} 2 & 3 & 4 \\ 9 & 1 & 5 \\ 8 & 7 & 6 \end{array}$$

MRS

$$\begin{array}{ccc} 6 & 7 & 8 \\ 5 & 1 & 9 \\ 4 & 3 & 2 \end{array} \quad \begin{array}{ccc} 2 & 3 & 4 \\ 9 & 1 & 5 \\ 8 & 7 & 6 \end{array}$$

Discrete MRs

6	7	8		11	12	13
5	1	9		18	10	14
4	3	2		17	16	15

MRS

33	34	35		20	21	22
32	28	36		27	19	23
31	30	29		26	25	24

Continuous MRs

Continuous MRSs

Discrete MRSs

Are you curious what these MRSs might actually look like in the extreme? Take the following images to be examples of what buildings in an artificial memory-city could potentially look like from the outside. Although perhaps exceptionally adorned with images, these are nevertheless indicative of the mnemonic creativity that can be applied in the creation of MRSs. Pay heed not only to the images decorating the surface, but also the general structure of these Hindu temples:

53

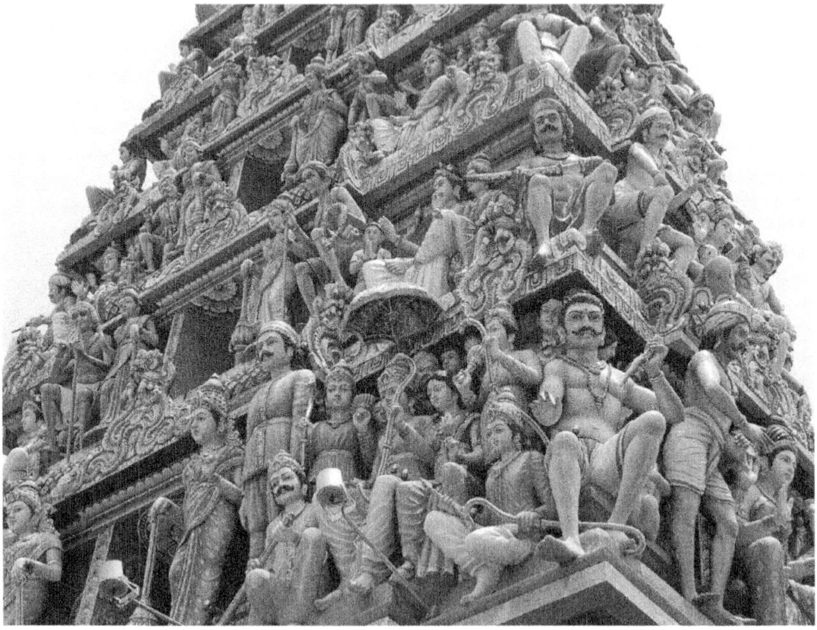

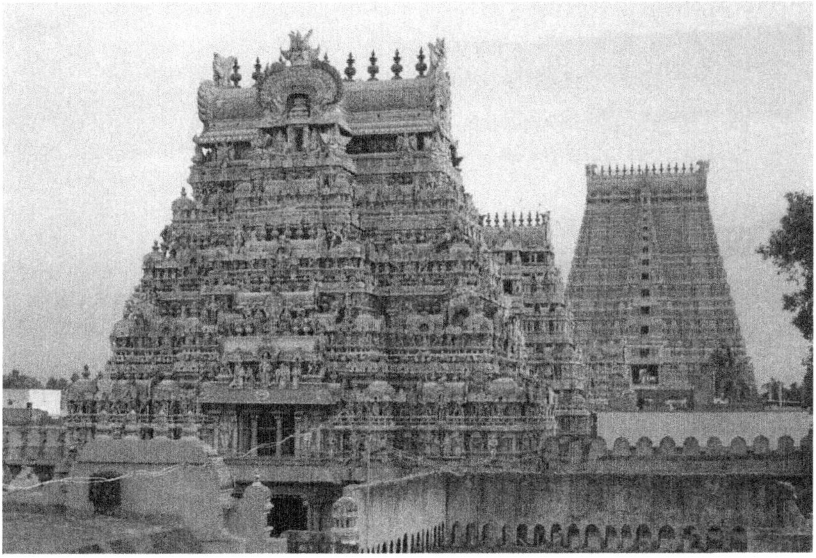

Key Terms:

Memory Location (ML): *A single location upon which an MU may be bound, as for example, a corner in a room, a piece of furniture, a window, a doorway, an external feature to some building, or any other distinct object or unified set of objects (Note that MUs, when other MUs are bound to them, are essentially the same as MLs).*

Memory Room (MR): *A set of MLs confined in some kind of distinct, compartmentalized area, as for example, a walled room, a small garden, or a car.*

Memory Room System (MRS): *A set of MRs usually sequential in order.*

Massive Memory Room System (mMRS): *Any MRS composed of multiple MRSs. The "level" of MRS is denoted by an exponent to the right of the term.*

Memory Field (MF): *A mnemonic area consisting of a set of one or more MLs, MRs, MRSs, or mMRSs.*

Method of Loci (or Loci Method): *The Mnemonic Device that takes advantage of the human sense of space. In this technique, symbolic images, or "MUs (Mnemonic Units)," are bound to spatially distinct and sequentially ordered mental locations called MLs (Memory Locations).*

Mnemograph: *A detailed illustration of a memory field, showing all MRs, MRSs, and mMRSs, as well as depicting and describing all MLs and potentially all MUs bound therein and their arrangements. Essentially, a memory field blueprint.*

Part 9 | Sequence, Order, and Category

Let us discuss the Art of Memory as it pertains to the necessity and utility of sequence, order, and category in the placement of MUs, MRs, and MRSs.

Now, there is certainly information out there which you may find yourself needing or wanting to recall in a specific order or sequence. Furthermore, for organizational purposes, it is highly likely that the information you want to memorize is in some way categorical. For example, you may want to memorize an entire English dictionary, to recall on a moment's notice the exact page and line of every single word in the English language. Or perhaps you need to remember a specific set of terms for your upcoming chemistry or physiology midterm such that each and every term has its associated MU bound in some fashion to an MUN of some more general term. Likewise, you might want to organize your memory according to the chapters and headings of the physics or biology textbook that you are currently studying. If such is the case, the next technique of the Art of Memory is going to be extremely useful to you; it is not an exaggeration to say that it is in fact quite possible to memorize an entire dictionary by creatively applying the following mnemonic device. So, generally speaking, this next method shall be very useful for memorizing any list of terms that have sequence, order, and or category. It is as Aristotle says: "*For, in order of succession, the mnemonic movements are to one another as the objective facts (from which they are derived). Accordingly, things arranged in a fixed order, like the successive demonstrations in geometry, are easy to remember (or recollect) while badly arranged subjects are not remembered with difficulty.*"(8) That is, if we desire to remember some information, we should first search for some inherent order within it, and subsequently arrange our MUs by some means that would allow us to infer that information's inherent order. Let us define a single instance of "movement" from one ML to another, from one MU to another, or from one MU to an ML and vice versa, as a *Mnemonic Jump* and a series of these as a *Mnemonic Journey*. Both of these are similarly termed as *Mnemonic Movement*.

There is made no distinction between "jumping" from one ML to another ML, and from one MU to another MU, because MUs and MLs are substantially the same, but an MU suggests symbolism whereas an ML suggests relative position. Likewise, once an MU has been attached to an ML, it inherently gains locality as a component of the particular MLs memory field and can therefore merge to become an ML itself. In other words, there is no restriction suggesting that an ML cannot have symbolic content and vice versa. Let us define this transformation from MU to ML as the process of *Angulation*. Furthermore, the process of angulation begs the questions: To what ML is the first angulation of a memory system relative in a being that has yet to form a memory field at all, as is with a newborn? And: Is there an inherent (and or perhaps inherited?) memory field that we are all born with? Likewise, the distinction between moving through MU linkages as opposed to moving according to the spatial sequentially of MLs is that the former does not require angularity.

Aristotle, on the subject of Mnemonic Movement: *"If this order be necessary, whenever a subject experiences the former of two movements thus connected, it will (invariably) experience the latter; if, however, the order be not necessary, but customary, only in the majority of cases will the subject experience the latter of the two movements. But it is a fact that there are some movements, by a single experience of which persons take the impress of custom more deeply than they do by experiencing others many times; hence upon seeing some things but once we remember them better than others which we may have been frequently."*(9)

By this it is meant that it is not enough to have one MU acting upon another, devoid of reciprocation or reaction, but that the one so affected by the particular act must show the associated effect. In our example depicting the several MUs for the parts of a Eukaryotic cell, this means that we should, for example, have the little girl show that she received the pat on the head by having her show some sign of discontent at that act, or that we should notice the woman respond to being bitten by the dinosaur by attempting to pull her leg away. This process is termed *Linking*. Thus, for every causality of some series of MUs linked by actions or relations of a sort, if we desire to remember them in conglomeration, ordered or not, we must always show in some creative way how one receives another's nature. And this reception by means of nature need not always be by action and response, but by means of similarity, or likeness. For example, when by *milk* I remember *white*, and by white, a *sheep*, and by a sheep, a *farm*, and so on and so forth; but in my opinion, actions are more powerful than likeness in linking MUs, but such symmetries of nature should not be disregarded by the practitioner when connecting images. Instead this should be considered as a valuable part of the mnemonic repertoire.

Key Terms:

Mnemonic Order: *A non-arbitrary arrangement of memory locations in space.*

Mnemonic Sequence: *An non-arbitrary arrangement in time. Essentially Sequence is Order in time.*

Linking: *The process of creating a causal relation between two MUs, two MLs, or an MU and an ML, as for example, when we imagine one MU interacting physically or intentionally sharing a similar property with another MU. Furthermore, the actual link formed, the relationship between the MUs and MLs, is known as a "linkage."*

Mnemonic Jump: *The cognitive movement of recollection from one MU or ML to another.*

Mnemonic Journey: *A series of mnemonic jumps; a series of cognitive movements of recollection through a set of MUs and or MLs.*

Mnemonic Movement: *A movement from one ML or MU to another through its linkage. Both mnemonic jumps and mnemonic journeys are mnemonic movement.*

Angulation: *That act of transforming an MU into an ML through envisioning its specific angularity relative to other memory fields including other singular MLs.*

Part 10 | The Method of Loci Continued

Returning to the topic of sequence and order, the reasons for needing this in the memory-city should now be obvious: it is highly likely that if you are memorizing some information, of any kind, that such information is either already sequential and ordered and needs to be memorized as such, or that the information you need to memorize would benefit from such sequence and order.

So sequence and order are valuable to us because, upon their implementation, we are enabled to remember the location of some MU, and therefore its implied term or meaning by virtue of its spatial relationship with other objects of memory. For example, let's say that you have four locations, A, B, C, and D, in the four lower corners of a square room. And let us assume that they have the order of *A-B-C-D*:

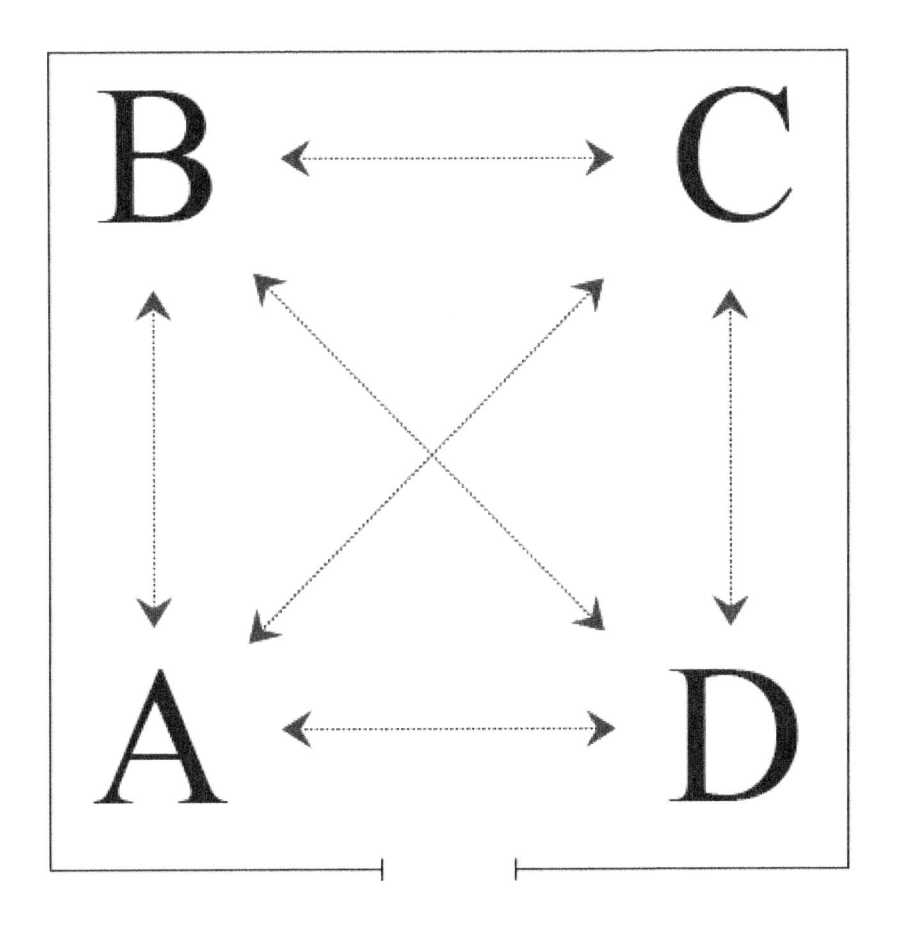

Therefore, by knowing where we are spatially in relation to one letter, we subsequently know where the other's locations must be. Thus, through simple inference we may determine the location of whichever MU has been bound to a particular letter according to the predetermined order of the room. If we apply this concept to some story or novel, for example, this point can be illustrated further: Given some general rule for sequence, say that your first and consecutive places always proceed clockwise. Then, in the first position, let's use our *A-B-C-D* MR, where at *A* we place an MU that very generally symbolizes the events that occur in the first chapter, and so on and so forth around the room for the next three chapters, binding their respective MUs to those locations. Thusly we may infer that each MU in the sequence of places must necessarily imply the sequence inherent in the structure of something with natural order, as with chaptered books. That is, the mMRSs, MRSs, MRs, MLs, MUNs, and MUs may become symbolic reflections of the order and sequence in whatever information you desire to remember.

This concept can be similarly applied to singular MUs, especially when they have humanoids or animals as their central image as, for example, when we allot numerical sequence to their various body parts.

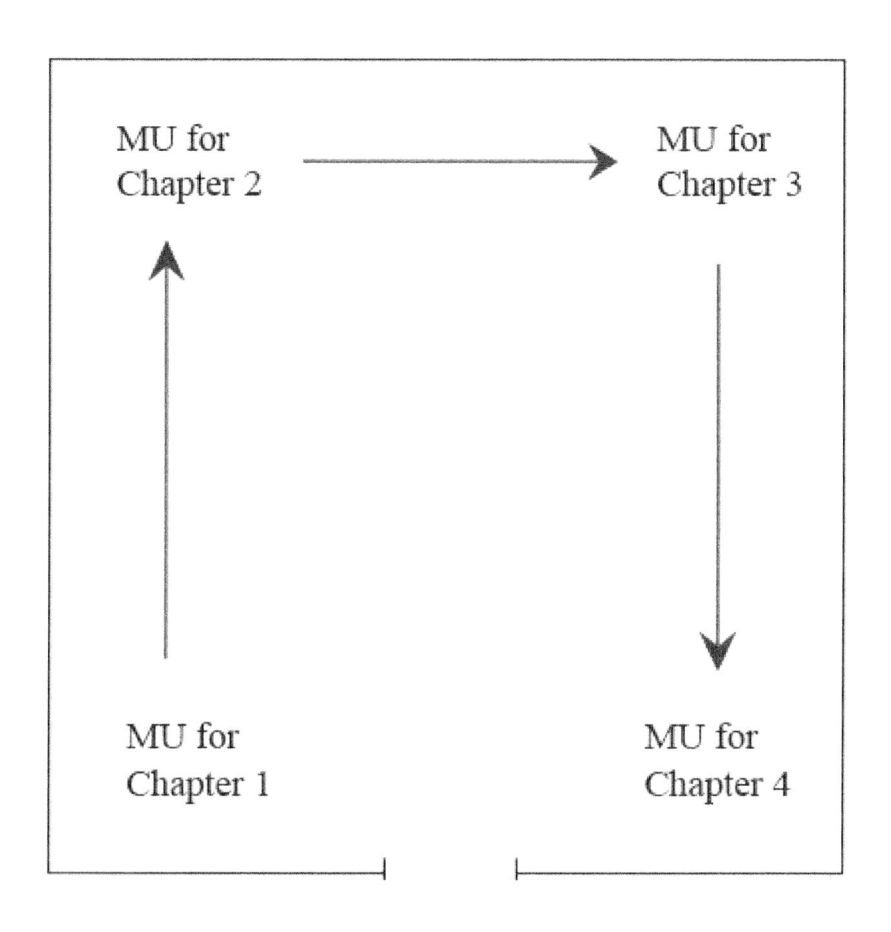

```
MU for           ────────▶    MU for
Chapter 2                     Chapter 3
   ▲                             │
   │                             │
   │                             ▼
MU for                        MU for
Chapter 1                     Chapter 4
```

Part 11 | A Small Universe and the Practical Application of the Method of Loci

It is quite possible that someone reading this book is a college student and that over the course of their college career they will probably take upwards of fifty different courses across dozens of subjects. These individuals will likely need to memorize thousands of terms for the various subjects they are studying. But how can they confidently and permanently retain all of that novel information? Wouldn't it be helpful to have a means by which one could very quickly, effectively, and with great permanence store vast amounts of information in their brain for future recall? This current section as well as the next will focus on a memory technique that will allow anyone to do just that. This technique is the ultimate application of the principles of the Method of Loci and the Alphabets. If this technique is implemented properly and with genuine effort you will then likely have a memory much greater than any of your peers, and really most individuals on the planet, except those efficiently practicing similar techniques. In other words, a truly genius-level memory.

Now, there are four ways by which we may form our MRSs. The first means is by using locations which actually exist during our waking physical existences. Secondly, we may imagine entirely new universes, worlds, cities, buildings, locations, etc. Thirdly, we may create something entirely otherworldly in nature to use as the basis for our binding of MUs. And fourthly, we may use some combination of the aforementioned.

For MRSs based upon waking locations, would it not be reasonable to draw from your own experiences when determining which cities and locations you will use to form the basis for the binding of memory images? For example, you may choose the city you were born in as your first MRS^2. And in this memory-city you could choose ten areas which are well known to you in terms of location, shape, and appearance. An example of such an area in your home city might be your actual house. Subsequently, you may visually break up your home into a great many individuated floors, MRs and MLs, however many there are, which you would then categorize as necessary by the placement of room-signifying MUs. This concept is perfectly encapsulated in a quote by Ramon Llull: *The memory is carried out in two ways, namely by means of places and images. Places do not differ from images except that places are not corners, as some people think, but certain kinds of fixed images*(10) *on which delible images are written, as if on paper. Thus places are like matter and images like form… However it is necessary that these places have clear boundaries, and that the distance between them is neither too long nor too short, but moderate distances, such as five feet or so; neither should it be too bright or too dark but moderately lit… You should choose, therefore, if you can, a particular house with twenty-two different and dissimilar rooms… and you should always have these places fixed in your mind's eye as they are positioned in the rooms, and you should know how to recite from them backwards and forwards in turn, and know what comes first, what comes second, what comes third and so on... If some familiar name is given to you to remember, for example 'John,' take a John known to you... and you will put [the image of] him in a place.*(11)

Now, for example, if you are desirous of memorizing all of the different amino acids for your upcoming chemistry midterm, we should place at the entrance or at the center of some MR in your home an MU symbolizing the term "Amino Acid" (the designation by the MUN of a plural quantity of the subjects is not necessary). This MU is subsequently considered a MUN and should then be, in some way, bound to all of the MUs for the various amino acids, either by likeness, activity, relation, sequence, or a combination of these. Similarly, you may perhaps wish to designate a particular MRS as the area wherein you store all of your MUs that symbolize the great quantity of terminology in your biology textbook. In such a case, you will therefore likely need to form a great number of MUNs to symbolize the various categories within that vast science. Because of this, we must create some way to hierarchically distinguish between MUNs, as least terminologically. So, we shall define MUNs as having an α and β distinction – that is, a less general and more general distinction. However, please remember that every MU can potentially be a MUN for other MUs. Therefore, the α and β distinction serves to designate only relative, categorical magnitudes between two MUs, one being directly subordinate, or less general (the βMUN), and the other superordinate, that is directly superior and more general (the αMUN). Furthermore, we may again apply the ^2 and ^3 symbolism to denote the actual MUN level relative to the entire hierarchy of MUs. For example, our MU for the term *Cellular Biology* would be our highest MUN without any exponential significations. Our next most general term might be *Eukaryotic Cells*. This MUN would be given the signification of MUN^2. Again, *Mitochondria* would be an MUN^3. Even further down the chain, the MU for the fact that Mitochondria have their *own DNA* (Mitochondrial DNA) would be designated as a MUN^4, and so on and so forth. Therefore, we would term the MUN^2 symbolizing the term "Eukaryotic Cells" as the αMUN relative to the MUN^3 symbolizing "Mitochondria," which is the βMUN.

The second method involves the creation of an entire universe, and by universe I mean a history – a world. In this world, it is then possible to create an infinite number of locations. For example, you may create a world as vast as J.R.R. Tolkien's *Lord of the Rings*. The options for creativity in this regard are limitless. An interesting thing about this method is that you can actually populate this world with, in a way, living characters that can be interacted with and have their own personal stories. Although such a technique is not restricted to only this method, it seems quite fitting. The Art of Memory in this context truly exemplifies the human imagination and creative faculty functioning at its zenith, at least in regard to activities restricted to the mind.

The third method involves the creation of a memory-city wherein the base MRSs are often confined to either abstract three dimensional shapes or novel structures based upon real architecture. An example of this would be Giordano Bruno's Atria(12). Other types of architecture which lend themselves easily to memory binding are columned Greek, Roman, and Egyptian temples.

The fourth method usually combines the artificial with the real, although a triple combination is possible. This method is almost perfectly exemplified in a very beautiful painting by Giovanni Paolo shown later in the book. In this method, we bind real locations to paintings and orderly place them into an MRS. This greatly lowers the amount of mental space necessary for storing memories.

However, please note that MRSs, need not be enclosed buildings, but can also be open spaces such as beaches and gardens. And the same is true of MRs, which can be "outside" as well.

Are you curious as to what an artificial memory-city might look like? The photos on the next pages show Plato's ideal city, which is a representation of what an artificial memory-city can look like at the magnitude of MRS^2 or MRS^3. It is important to note the highly geometrical nature of the cities within these images. This kind of geometric sectioning enables easy categorization of major topics and even entire sciences. Can you imagine storing every single fact, term, and definition you have ever learned in a highly geometric, and philosophically significant, memory-city like this? Truly amazing!

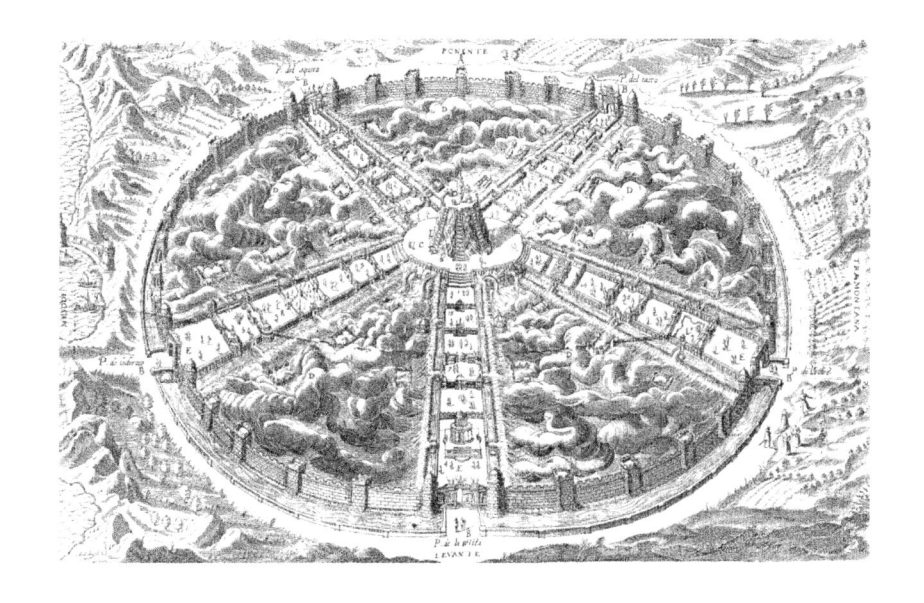

*Two Depictions of Plato's Ideal City

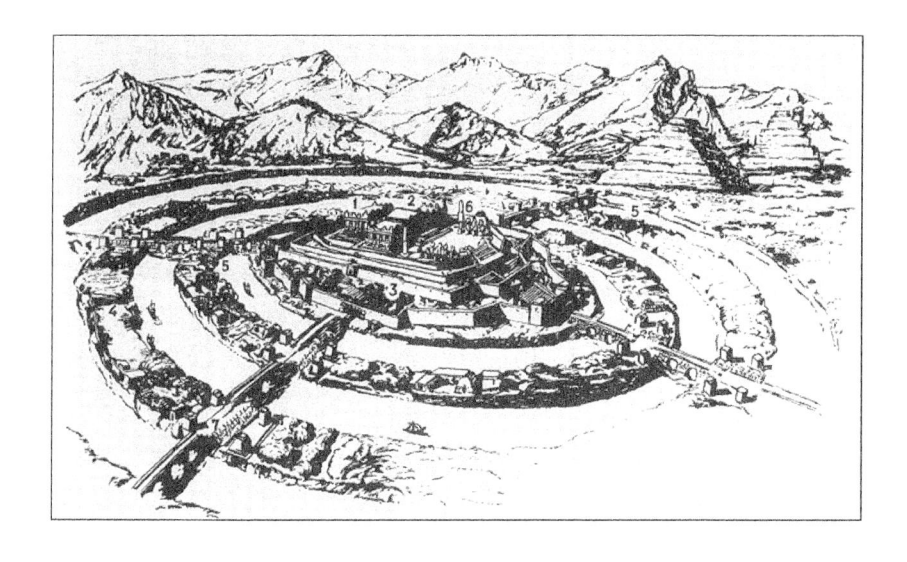

Part 12 | A Major Example

A major example is now given using a combination of the preceding mnemonic techniques for the memorization of the one hundred and eighteen elements of the Periodic Table of Elements. Note, however, that the numerical sequence of the elements deviates from their categories when ordered according to atomic number. For example, Hydrogen and Helium, the first and second elements respectively, belong to different groups. Categorization of these groups is therefore secondarily defined using MUCs. That is, the MUs for each element of a particular category will have a similar MUC to denote the group they belong to. That is, its sympathetic or analogous nature as it pertains to one of the nine Aristotelian categories. These groups within the Periodic Table of Elements, of which there are ten, may each be defined by a MUN, which will be mnemonically bound to the subjects of the group by means of a common nature. If you wish, you may further describe each of the elements with MUs for their atomic masses or electronegativity, but this is not done here. The process for these will be the same as for the Elements themselves but instead of each atomic mass or electronegativity MU being bound in series to each other, they will be first bound to their associated element's MU. As you can tell, the amount of information to be potentially memorized here is vast, but no matter whom you are, with the proper application of mnemonics, the completion of this task becomes greatly easier.

For our MRS, to store this vast quantity and for the sake of ease of exemplification, we will use five twenty-fourths of the foundational atria and backgrounds of a certain famous Brunic memory-city. (13) However, the reader should understand that only a portion of the city is given here because we only wish to show how to apply all of our memory techniques to MRSs, rather than exemplify an entire memory-city at this time. This five twenty-fourths portion is constituted by five atriums with five major backgrounds; each of these atria are themselves composed of twenty four MLs each. The following diagram depicts these five atria, their cardinal points, and their multiple backgrounds. These Atria, for now, should be envisioned as being in parallel.

East Corner	East	South Corner
North	Image of the Atrium	South
North Corner	West	West Corner

1. Water		4. Bath	7. Palm
2. Plow	4*	5. Breastplate	8. Anchor
3. Chain		6. Amphora	9. Chariot
1*			
22. Desk		10. Stable
23. Skiff	*Altar*	11. Fruit
24. Throne		12. Smoke
19. Prison	16. Oven	13. Tree
20. Jar	17. Sword	14. Globe
21. Stool	18. Fire	15. Banquet

25. Pool 26. Relics 27. Offering	28. Hotsprings 29. Stool 30. Treasures	31. Desert 32. Mirage 33. Delight
46. Furies 47. Bottles 48. Hoe	*Basilica*	34. Horn 35. Badge 36. Bason
43. Inferno 44. Dragon 45. Yoke	40. Camal 41. Quiver 42. Box	37. Lantern 38. Ghost 39. Bier

49. Noose 50. Handcuffs 51. Snake	52. Parrot 53. Guitar 54. Axe	55. Bridge 56. Cloud 57. Maniple
70. Dung 71. Snow 72. Bearskin	*Prison*	58. Bracelet 59. Harp 60. Compass
67. Ghost 68. Basket 69. Fan	64. Dirt 65. Frogs 66. Old woman	61. Old man 62. Specter 63. Mud

73. Coal 74. Ash 75. Bellow	76. Key 77. Icon 78. Flute	79. Dog 80. Canister 81. Figurine
94. Hair 95. Owl 96. Tree	*House*	82. Sword 83. Spur 84. Dog
91. Clock 92. Lagoon 93. Nail	88. Hook 89. Cat 90. Shrine	85. Cat 86. Tile 87. Platter

97. Wine 98. Javelin 99. Thorns	100. Flies 101. Linen 102. Shield	103. Fillet 104. Knife 105. Bone
118. Fork 119. Net 120. Fish	*Colt*	106. Gavel 107. Book 108. Stone
115. Butter 116. Square 117. Muzzle	112. Garland 113. Axe 114. Club	109. Dart 110. Rose 111. Gem

*These atria are modified versions of Bruno's originals. For ease of exemplification and understanding, the total order and some natures of the backgrounds have been modified. A complete exposition of Bruno's memory-city is to be given in a later book.

In this system, each set of three backgrounds of the one hundred and twenty MLs is to be conformed into a single MU; these sets of three in themselves do not take into account the total sequence of MLs from one to one hundred and twenty. Instead, these are grouped as such for the sake of defining certain discrete areas of their respective atria. In other words, each set of three backgrounds defines one of eight angles – a quasi MR, and these are the cardinal directions including their middle angles. The total sequence, on the other hand, is to be implied by the causal relationships between each of the MUs for the elements placed upon the backgrounds.

Each of the particular backgrounds for each ML do have an inherent number, but it is not necessary to make such a distinction in their combined MU. However, each MU will be allotted to one of these backgrounds according to its order in the entire system. Thus, we have five atria total, each defined by one background, forty angles defined by forty groups of three backgrounds, and one hundred and twenty sequential backgrounds for the binding of our one hundred and eighteen MUs of the elements. Furthermore, please note that the causation between the multitude of MUs is sufficient for their total remembrance, but that we include the backgrounds and the atriums designed according to the Method of Loci because we wish to show how the several techniques may be combined to improve our recollection of the MUs and to show their sequence.

Each of these techniques is useful on its own, but in combination with each other are superior to themselves individually. Nevertheless, the memory will become exalted in relation to your peers even if the Method of Loci is excluded from the recipe. As was stated before, the Method of Loci enables the remembrance of order and number, and the way in which the rooms are divided makes it easier to find the number of a particular MU in a sequence of MUs because of multiplication. That is, in a series of MRs, each composed of ten MLs, the second MR in the series necessarily begins with the eleventh ML, and the third, the twenty-first, and so on. Whereas, if we only knew the number of an MU by its relation with other MUs, we will likely be forced to count till we arrive at the ML we want. In analogy, if we were to observe a great string of numbers, say one hundred of them, randomized, it would be difficult to pinpoint which is the seventy seventh, or thirteenth, or fifty-ninth, etc., without first counting to that place. This issue is alleviated through sectioning or, in this example, counting by numbers greater than one. When mnemonics is applied to visual data (MUs), the sectioning task is accomplished using the Method of Loci. Therefore, this method is invaluable when dealing with the MUs for large and innately sequential quantities of ordered terms, such as in the Elements of the Periodic Table.

Furthermore, normally the backgrounds would partake in some way of the nature of the atria themselves, as they usually do in real life. For example, in the atria of the prison, each of the backgrounds would be ones which might be commonly found in a prison or have some natural association with a prison. This is to enable the recollection of which atria the particular MU, bound to the particular background, is located just by observing its nature. Similarly, each of the backgrounds – their own names – should be alphabetically chosen so as to enable the quick recognition of the specific number of the particular MUs bound to them. Although alphabetization of backgrounds is not necessary and will likely greatly task your personal lexicon, it is particularly helpful to do so when you are first learning which background belongs to which location.

Our MUs, their associated Elements, and atomic order are as follows:

Atrium of the Altar

1 - H – Hydrogen – HI-DR: In the 1st place of the Atrium of the Altar, symbolizing the Element of Hydrogen, arises the image of a *beehive being played upon by a drummer balancing a bucket of water on his head.*
2 - He – Helium – HE-LE: In the 2st place of the Atrium of the Altar, symbolizing the Element of Helium, arises the image of a *hen laying lemons being swept away by a plow.*
3 - Li – Lithium – LIT-H: In the 3rd place of the Atrium of the Altar, symbolizing the Element of Lithium, arises the image of a *man holding a lighter burning hair with a chain wrapped around his neck, choking him.*
4 - Be – Beryllium – BARREL: In the 4th place of the Atrium of the Altar, symbolizing the Element of Beryllium, arises the image of a *beautiful woman taking a bath pouring water upon herself from a large barrel.*
5 - B – Boron – BO-RO: In the 5th place of the Atrium of the Altar, symbolizing the Element of Boron, arises the image of a *boxer balancing on a large boulder while wearing a breastplate*
6 - C – Carbon – CAR: In the 6th place of the Atrium of the Altar, symbolizing the Element of Carbon, arises the image of a *car smashing into a priceless amphora.*
7 - N – Nitrogen – NI-TR: In the 7th place of the Atrium of the Altar, symbolizing the Element of Nitrogen, arises the image of a *ninja swinging on a trapeze hanging between two palm trees.*
8 - O – Oxygen – OX: In the 8th place of the Atrium of the Altar, symbolizing the Element of Oxygen, arises the image of an *ox pulling an anchor.*
9 - F – Fluorine – FL-RE: In the 9th place of the Atrium of the Altar, symbolizing the Element of Fluorine, arises the image of a *redneck playing the flute while riding a chariot.*
10 - Ne – Neon – NE-ON: In the 10th place of the Atrium of the Altar, symbolizing the Element of Neon,

arises the image of a *scholar eating raw onions while sitting in a stable.*

11 - Na – Sodium – SO-D: In the 11th place of the Atrium of the Altar, symbolizing the Element of Sodium, arises the image of a *soccer player slipping on fruit while trying to kick a dove.*

12 - Mg – Magnesium – MAG-NE: In the 12th place of the Atrium of the Altar, symbolizing the Element of Magnesium, arises the image of a *mage smoking a pipe from his neck.*

13 - Al – Aluminum – AL-UM: In the 13th place of the Atrium of the Altar, symbolizing the Element of Aluminum, arises the image of a *beautiful woman climbing a tree while carrying a luggage bag filled with alarm clocks.*

14 - Si – Silicon – SI-LI: In the 14th place of the Atrium of the Altar, symbolizing the Element of Silicon, arises the image of a *Siamese twins burning a globe with a lighter.*

15 - P – Phosphorus – FA-FO: In the 15th place of the Atrium of the Altar, symbolizing the Element of Phosphorus, arises the image of a *falcon grabbing a fox that was stealing food from a banquet.*

16 - S – Sulfur – SURFER: In the 16th place of the Atrium of the Altar, symbolizing the Element of Sulfur, arises the image of a *surfer faux riding an oven.*

17 - Cl – Chlorine – CL-RE: In the 17th place of the Atrium of the Altar, symbolizing the Element of Helium, arises the image of *clown wielding a sword and riding a dinosaur.*

18 - Ar – Argon – AR-G: In the 18tht place of the Atrium of the Altar, symbolizing the Element of Argon, arises the image of an *archer shooting a flaming arrow at a gorilla.*

19 - K – Potassium – PO-SE: In the 19th place of the Atrium of the Altar, symbolizing the Element of Potassium, arises the image of a *beautiful woman wearing prisoner's clothing and spilling a bag of potatoes while riding a large seahorse.*

20 - Ca – Calcium – CA-L: In the 20th place of the Atrium of the Altar, symbolizing the Element of Calcium, arises the image of a *lion biting into an aluminum while stuck in a jar*

21 - Sc – Scandium – SC-N-DI: In the 21st place of the Atrium of the Altar, symbolizing the Element of Scandium, arises the image of a *scorpion covered in diamond, on a stool and trapped by a net*.

22 - Ti – Titanium – TI-TA: In the 22nd place of the Atrium of the Altar, symbolizing the Element of Titanium, arises the image of a *tire balanced on a table on top of a desk*.

23 - V – Vanadium – V-N-AD: In the 23rd place of the Atrium of the Altar, symbolizing the Element of Vanadium, arises the image of a *vulture, a naked woman, and an admiral in a small skiff*.

24 - Cr – Chromium – CR-MI In the 24th place of the Atrium of the Altar, symbolizing the Element of Chromium, arises the image of a *crab wearing oven mittens sitting on a throne*.

Atrium of the Basilica

25 - Mn – Manganese – MAN-GA: In the 1st place of the Atrium of the Basilica, symbolizing the Element of Manganese, arises the image of a *man jumping a gazelle into a pool*.

26 - Fe – Iron – I-RO: In the 2rd place of the Atrium of the Basilica, symbolizing the Element of Iron, arises the image of a *robot crucified upon the Cross with an eyeball in each palm*.

27 - Co – Cobalt – CO-BA: In the 3rd place of the Atrium of the Basilica, symbolizing the Element of Cobalt, arises the *image of a baby drinking from the utter of a cow that has had its throat cut*.

28 - Ni – Nickel – NI-CL: In the 4th place of the Atrium of the Basilica, symbolizing the Element of Nickel, arises the image of a *ninja relaxing in a hot spring while holding a clock above his head*.

29 - Cu – Copper – CO-PR: In the 5th place of the Atrium of the Basilica, symbolizing the Element of Copper, arises the image of a *professor standing on burning coals instead of sitting on an empty stool next to him*.

30 - Zn – Zinc – Z-IN: In the 6th place of the Atrium of the Basilica, symbolizing the Element of Zinc, arises the image of a *zebra drawing stripes upon himself using ink while coveting treasure*.

31 - Ga – Gallium – GA-LE: In the 7th place of the Atrium of the Basilica, symbolizing the Element of Gallium, arises the image of a *gangster covered in leeches while succumbing to the heat of the desert*.

32 - Ge – Germanium – GERMAN: In the 8th place of the Atrium of the Basilica, symbolizing the Element of Germanium, arises the image of a *German man holding a magicians hat*.

33 - As – Arsenic – AR-SE: In the 9th place of the Atrium of the Basilica, symbolizing the Element of Arsenic, arises the image of *two settlers carrying the Ark of the*

Covenant, exuding great happiness for the act.

34 - Se – Selenium – SELENE: In the 10th place of the Atrium of the Basilica, symbolizing the Element of Selenium, arises the image of a *moon goddess holding a large goat's horn.*

35 - Br – Bromine – BR-ME: In the 11th place of the Atrium of the Basilica, symbolizing the Element of Bromine, arises the image of a *brain on a plate next to a plate of meat and a police officer's badge between them.*

36 - Kr – Krypton – CR-P: In the 12th place of the Atrium of the Basilica, symbolizing the Element of Krypton, arises the image of several *purple crows drinking from the edge of a large water-filled basin.*

37 - Rb – Rubidium – RUBY: In the 13th place of the Atrium of the Basilica, symbolizing the Element of Rubidium, arises the image of a *ruby emitting red light from the inside of a lantern.*

38 - Sr – Strontium – STRONG: In the 14th place of the Atrium of the Basilica, symbolizing the Element of Strontium, arises the image of a *ghost scaring a strong man.*

39 - Y – Yttrium – Y-TR: In the 15th place of the Atrium of the Basilica, symbolizing the Element of Yttrium, arises the image of a large *yak swinging on a trapeze above a bier.*

40 - Zr – Zirconium – Z-R-CO: In the 16th place of the Atrium of the Basilica, symbolizing the Element of Zirconium, arises the image of a *czar holding a rake in one hand and a copper wire in the other while riding a camel.*

41 - Nb – Niobium – NI-O-BE: In the 17th place of the Atrium of the Basilica, symbolizing the Element of Niobium, arises the image of the *pregnant goddess Nike with an owl sitting on her belly and a quiver of arrows around her shoulder.*

42 - Mo – Molybdenum – MO-LE-B: In the 18th place of the Atrium of the Basilica, symbolizing the Element of Molybdenum, arises the image of *Mozart fighting a leopard and using a baguette as a weapon, and protecting a box.*

43 - Tc – Technetium – TE-C-N: In the 19th place of

the Atrium of the Basilica, symbolizing the Element of Technetium, arises the image of a *chemist handing a teddy bear to a neanderthal while standing in an inferno.*

44 - Ru – Ruthenium – RU-TH: In the 20th place of the Atrium of the Basilica, symbolizing the Element of Ruthenium, arises the image of a *rugby player riding a dragon and waving thong in the air.*

45 - Rh – Rhodium – RO-D: In the 21st place of the Atrium of the Basilica, symbolizing the Element of Rhodium, arises the image of a *doctor with a yoke around his neck holding a rose.*

46 - Pd – Palladium – PA-LA: In the 22nd place of the Atrium of the Basilica, symbolizing the Element of Palladium, arises the image of a *woman holding a cooking pan, surrounded by the Two Furies.*

47 - Ag – Silver – SILVER: In the 23rd place of the Atrium of the Basilica, symbolizing the Element of Silver, arises the image a *woman measuring wine from a wine bottle into a silver spoon.*

48 - Cd – Cadmium – CADDY: In the 24th place of the Atrium of the Basilica, symbolizing the Element of Cadmium, arises the image of a *caddy swinging a hoe as if it were a golf club.*

Atrium of the Prison

49 - In – Indium – INDIAN: In the 1st place of the Atrium of the Prison, symbolizing the Element of Indium, arises the image of an *Indian woman with a noose around her neck.*

50 - Sn – Tin – TIN: In the 2nd place of the Atrium of the Prison, symbolizing the Element of Tin, arises the image of a *handcuffed woman holding a tin can.*

51 - Sb – Antimony – ANT-MO: In the 3rd place of the Atrium of the Prison, symbolizing the Element of Antimony, arises the image of a *snake consuming a mouse and being swarmed by ants.*

52 - Te – Tellurium – TEL-LU: In the 4th place of the Atrium of the Prison, symbolizing the Element of Tellurium, arises the image of a *woman using a telephone covered in fishing lures and being hooked by them, with a parrot on her shoulder.*

53 - I – Iodine – I-OD: In the 5th place of the Atrium of the Prison, symbolizing the Element of Iodine, arises the image of an *eyeless Odin playing the guitar.*

54 - Xe – Xenon – X-NO: In the 6th place of the Atrium of the Prison, symbolizing the Element of Xenon, arises the image of a *mathematician pointing to his nose and swinging an axe.*

55 - Cs – Cesium – C-Z: In the 7th place of the Atrium of the Prison, symbolizing the Element of Cesium, arises the image of a *zebra striped cat crossing a bridge.*

56 - Ba – Barium – BEAR: In the 8th place of the Atrium of the Prison, symbolizing the Element of Barium, arises the image of a *bear resting on a cloud.*

57 - La – Lanthanum – LA-N-TH: In the 9th place of the Atrium of the Prison, symbolizing the Element of Lanthanum, arises the image of a *lawyer have a nail hammered into his throat by a roman soldier.*

58 - Ce – Cerium – C-RE: In the 10th place of the Atrium of the Prison, symbolizing the Element of Cerium, arises the image of a *redneck coveting a beautiful bracelet and lying in a pile of cash.*

59 - Pr – Praseodymium – PR-CE-DI: In the 11th place of the Atrium of the Prison, symbolizing the Element of Praseodymium, arises the image of a *woman praying before a CEO holding a pair of die in one hand and leaning against a large harp.*

60 - Nd – Neodymium – NE-O-DI: In the 12th place of the Atrium of the Prison, symbolizing the Element of Neodymium, arises the image of a *scholar holding a compass and standing next to an old man holding a large diamond.*

61 - Pm – Promethium – PR-O-ME: In the 13th place of the Atrium of the Prison, symbolizing the Element of Promethium, arises the image of a *prisoner using a cane standing beside an old man holding a piece of meat.*

62 - Sm – Samarium – SA-MA-R: In the 14th place of the Atrium of the Prison, symbolizing the Element of Samarium, arises the image of a *large salmon being roasted by a freemason with Death observing.*

63 - Eu – Europium – U-OP: In the 15th place of the Atrium of the Prison, symbolizing the Element of Europium, arises the image of *yourself holding covered in mud and holding a brilliant opal.*

64 - Gd – Gadolinium – GA-DO-LI: In the 16th place of the Atrium of the Prison, symbolizing the Element of Gadolinium, arises the image of a *gangster riding a donkey, drinking liquor, and falling off the donkey onto the dirt.*

65 - Tb – Terbium – T-R-BE: In the 17th place of the Atrium of the Prison, symbolizing the Element of Terbium, arises the image of a *tailor covered in red paint, lying on a bed with a frog.*

66 - Dy – Dysprosium – DI-PR-SE: In the 18th place of the Atrium of the Prison, symbolizing the Element of Dysprosium, arises the image of a diver handing a *prism and a seashell to an old woman.*

67 - Ho – Holmium – HO-ME: In the 19th place of the Atrium of the Prison, symbolizing the Element of

Holmium, arises the image of a *hole filled with mercury and a ghoul rising out of it*.

68 - Er – Erbium – ER-BE: In the 20th place of the Atrium of the Prison, symbolizing the Element of Erbium, arises the image of *Eris carrying a basket of beans*.

69 - Tm – Thulium – TH-LE: In the 21st place of the Atrium of the Prison, symbolizing the Element of Thulium, arises the image of a *thief cooling a lemur using a fan*.

70 - Yb – Ytterbium – Y-TR-BE: In the 22nd place of the Atrium of the Prison, symbolizing the Element of Ytterbium, arises the image of a *yellow tractor crushing a beetle that was rolling some dung*.

71 - Lu – Lutetium – LUTE: In the 23rd place of the Atrium of the Prison, symbolizing the Element of Lutetium, arises the image of a *woman playing naked in the snow*.

72 - Hf – Hafnium – HA-F-NE: In the 24th place of the Atrium of the Prison, symbolizing the Element of Hafnium, arises the image of *Hades catching a woman by her necklace, using a fishing rod*.

Atrium of the House

73 - Ta – Tantalum – TA-N-TA: In the 1st place of the Atrium of the House, symbolizing the Element of Tantalum, arises the image of a *two tanned woman standing to the left and right of a Neanderthal, all standing on a bed of coals.*

74 - W – Tungsten – TONGUE: In the 2nd place of the Atrium of the House, symbolizing the Element of Tungsten, arises the image of a *woman placing lilac onto a pile of ash.*

75 - Re – Rhenium – R-E: In the 3rd place of the Atrium of the House, symbolizing the Element of Rhenium, arises the image of a *ronin using a below upon a pile of embers.*

76 - Os – Osmium – O-SM: In the 4th place of the Atrium of the House, symbolizing the Element of Osmium, arises the image of an *old man wearing a smock and holding a key.*

77 - Ir – Iridium – I-RI-D: In the 5th place of the Atrium of the House, symbolizing the Element of Iridium, arises the image of a *large eye, a river, and a searching detective holding a book.*

78 - Pt – Platinum – PL-TI: In the 6th place of the Atrium of the House, symbolizing the Element of Platinum, arises the image of a *plumber tiptoeing while playing the flute.*

79 - Au – Gold – GOLD: In the 7th place of the Atrium of the House, symbolizing the Element of Gold, arises the image of a *golden boy walking a dog.*

80 - Hg – Mercury – MERCURY: In the 8th place of the Atrium of the House, symbolizing the Element of Mercury, arises the image of a *beaker of mercury resting on a shelf.*

81 - Tl – Thallium – TH-AL: In the 9th place of the Atrium of the House, symbolizing the Element of Thallium, arises the image of an *alien with red thread wrapped around its right hand and almonds in its left, standing behind a small statue of a man.*

82 - Pb – Lead – L: In the 10th place of the Atrium of the House, symbolizing the Element of Lead, arises the image of a pile of *leafs surrounding a sword stuck into the ground.*
83 - Bi – Bismuth – BI-MU: In the 11th place of the Atrium of the House, symbolizing the Element of Bismuth, arises the image of a *musketeer wearing spurred boots, riding a bicycle.*
84 - Po – Polonium – POLO: In the 12th place of the Atrium of the House, symbolizing the Element of Polonium, arises the image of a *polo player on a horse chasing a dog.*
85 - At – Astatine – AS-TA-TE: In the 13th place of the Atrium of the House, symbolizing the Element of Astatine, arises the image of a *tennis player with her tennis racket taped to her hand trying to hit a cat, but instead her racket smashes into the asphalt.*
86 - Rn – Radon – RA-DO: In the 14th place of the Atrium of the House, symbolizing the Element of Radon, arises the image of a *white rabbit in the mouth of a dog with a knife beneath its paw.*
87 - Fr – Francium – FRANCE: In the 15th place of the Atrium of the House, symbolizing the Element of Francium, arises the image of a *French flag folded onto a silver platter.*
88 - Ra – Radium – RA-DE: In the 16th place of the Atrium of the House, symbolizing the Element of Radium, arises the image of a *rattlesnake squeezing a deer hanging from a hook.*
89 - Ac – Actinium – AC-TIN: In the 17th place of the Atrium of the House, symbolizing the Element of Actinium, arises the image of an *actor drinking from a soda can while holding a cat.*
90 - Th – Thorium – THOR: In the 18th place of the Atrium of the House, symbolizing the Element of Thorium, arises the image of *Thor kneeling before a shrine.*
91 - Pa – Protactinium – PR-TA-TI: In the 19th place of the Atrium of the House, symbolizing the Element of

Protactinium, arises the image of a *protestor standing before a tank and pointing to his watch*.

92 - U – Uranium – URANUS: In the 20th place of the Atrium of the House, symbolizing the Element of Uranium, arises the image of *Uranus standing near a lagoon, admiring the scenery*.

93 - Np – Neptunium – NEPTUNE: In the 21st place of the Atrium of the House, symbolizing the Element of Neptunium, arises the image of *Neptune in the process of being nailed to a cross*.

94 - Pu – Plutonium – PLUTO: In the 22nd place of the Atrium of the House, symbolizing the Element of Plutonium, arises the image of *PLUTO holding a woman's hair*.

95 - Am – Americium – AMERICA: In the 23rd place of the Atrium of the House, symbolizing the Element of Americium, arises the image of an *owl holding an American flag in its beak*.

96 - Cm – Curium – Q-RE: In the 24th place of the Atrium of the House, symbolizing the Element of Curium, arises the image of a *queen slapping a redneck that is hanging from tree*.

Atrium of the Colt

97 - Bk – Berkelium – BR-K-EL: In the 1st place of the Atrium of the Colt, symbolizing the Element of Berkelium, arises the image of a *bride playing with a kite, standing next to a king drinking wine.*

98 - Cf – Californium – CA-LI-FO: In the 2nd place of the Atrium of the Colt, symbolizing the Element of Californium, arises the image of a *Cardinal drinking from a liquor bottle while firing a musket at a fox.*

99 - Es – Einsteinium – EINSTEIN: In the 3rd place of the Atrium of the Colt, symbolizing the Element of Einsteinium, arises the image of *Einstein stuck in a thorny bush.*

100 - Fm – Fermium – FERMI: In the 4th place of the Atrium of the Colt, symbolizing the Element of Fermium, arises the image of *Fermi studying a jar of flies.*

101 - Md – Mendelevium – MENDELEEV: In the 5th place of the Atrium of the Colt, symbolizing the Element of Mendelevium, arises the image of *Mendeleev examining a jar of flies.*

102 - No – Nobelium – NOBEL: In the 6th place of the Atrium of the Colt, symbolizing the Element of Nobelium, arises the image of *Nobel holding a golden shield.*

103 - Lr – Lawrencium – LAWRENCE: In the 7th place of the Atrium of the Colt, symbolizing the Element of Lawrencium, arises the image of *Lawrence hiding beneath a piece of linen.*

104 - Rf – Rutherfordium – RU-TH-R: In the 8th place of the Atrium of the Colt, symbolizing the Element of Rutherfordium, arises the image of a *thug holding a red rudder and a knife.*

105 - Db – Dubnium – D-U-B: In the 9th place of the Atrium of the Colt, symbolizing the Element of Dubnium, arises the image of a *doctor eating a juicy piece of bacon with a fork while resting on a pile of bones.*

106 - Sg – Seaborgium – SEA-BORG: In the 10th place

of the Atrium of the Colt, symbolizing the Element of Seaborgium, arises the image of a *Borg steadily swimming in the sea while holding a judges gavel.*

107 - Bh – Bohrium – BOAR: In the 11th place of the Atrium of the Colt, symbolizing the Element of Bohrium, arises the image of a *boar reading a book.*

108 - Hs – Hassium – HA-SE: In the 12th place of the Atrium of the Colt, symbolizing the Element of Hassium, arises the image of a *harem of woman standing in the sea throwing stones at each other.*

109 - Mt – Meitnerium – ME-T-NE: In the 13th place of the Atrium of the Colt, symbolizing the Element of Meitnerium, arises the image of a *tailor with his measuring tape wrapped around the neck of a woman wearing a dartboard on her chest.*

110 - Ds – Darmstadtium – D-ARM-ST: In the 14th place of the Atrium of the Colt, symbolizing the Element of Darmstadtium, arises the image of a *dog with an arm in its mouth, standing on its hind legs. The hand of the arm holds a single red rose.*

111 - Rg – Roentgenium – RO-ENGINE: In the 15th place of the Atrium of the Colt, symbolizing the Element of Roentgenium, arises the image of a *Roman pouring a handful of gems into an engine.*

112 - Cn – Copernicium – CO-PR-NE: In the 16th place of the Atrium of the Colt, symbolizing the Element of Copernicium, arises the image of a *Copernicus wearing a garland.*

113 - Uut – Ununtrium – N-TR: In the 17th place of the Atrium of the Colt, symbolizing the Element of Ununtrium, arises the image of a *naked woman swinging from a trapeze while holding an axe.*

114 - Fl – Flerovium – FL-RO-V: In the 18th place of the Atrium of the Colt, symbolizing the Element of Flerovium, arises the image of a *Roman drinking from a flask while beating a vagrant with a club.*

115 - Uup – Ununpentium – N-PE: In the 19th place of

the Atrium of the Colt, symbolizing the Element of Ununpentium, arises the image of a *naked woman wearing pearls and eating butter*.
116 - Lv – Livermorium – LI-V-MO: In the 20th place of the Atrium of the Colt, symbolizing the Element of Livermorium, arises the image of a *vagrant man lighting the tale of a mouse on fire with a lighter*.
117 - Uus – Ununseptium – N-SE: In the 21st place of the Atrium of the Colt, symbolizing the Element of Ununseptium, arises the image of a *naked woman sewing while wearing a muzzle*.
118 - Uuo – Ununoctium – N-OC: In the 22nd place of the Atrium of the Colt, symbolizing the Element of Ununoctium, arises the image of a *naked woman eating an octopus with a fork*.

Having formed and memorized each of these images, the next task is to bind them to one another in sequence. For example, we should imagine the drummer of the MU for Hydrogen to be striking the chicken from the MU for Helium with a drumstick causing her to lay lemons. We could subsequently imagine the plow that strikes the chicken to continue on and trip the man choking himself, whom then falls over into the bath with the beautiful woman from the MU for Beryllium, extinguishing his hair in the water and greatly surprising her, and so on a so forth for each of the one hundred and eighteen MUs. Thus, we shall be enabled to find the name and atomic number of every Element as we follow the chain of causation between their MUs, either forward or backward, and from any starting location as long as we also pay heed to the sequence of their respective backgrounds.

As for our one hundred and twenty backgrounds specifically, we should combine them into groups of three according to the cardinal directions. This will make it easier to identify which backgrounds are located in which areas of the several atria. For example, we might create a conformed image of the first three backgrounds of the Atrium of the Altar, representing the East Corner by imagining the image of tractor dragging a man through water with a chain; this should then be the image that we recall first and will naturally elicit the recollection of the three MUs bound unto the three backgrounds that compose the image. And so on and so forth the mind's eye should proceed around the atria in sequence, drawing forth from each set of three backgrounds their associated MUs.

Any set of terms may be memorized in this way, sequential or otherwise, whether from your Chemistry, Physics, Biology, History, English, Engineering, Mechanics, or Mathematics course – no matter which subject – with the ultimate result of your obtaining very high marks in those classes. Furthermore, if one excels at this method and the alphabets and backgrounds being fully memorized, the rapid and complete memorization of terms, facts, and equations within the very lecture hall itself is possible, freeing up time for other passions and endeavors.

Next follows the images for the forty conjoined backgrounds describing the five atria; if you can, memorize these first – their specific sequence and locations. If you do so, you will have gained a very valuable and rare tool. These backgrounds may be similarly applied to the memorization of any information you desire to remember during your education, or afterwards, as may be required by circumstance:

In the **East Corner of the Atrium of the Altar**, arises the image of a *farmer driving a tractor, dragging a man through water with a chain.*

In the **East of the Atrium of the Altar**, arises the image of *beautiful woman washing a dirty breastplate with water she has drawn with an amphora from a bath.*

In the **South Corner of the Atrium of the Altar**, arises the image of *chariot pulling an anchor around a palm.*

In the **South of the Atrium of the Altar**, arises the image of *man carrying fruit from a smoking stable.*

In the **West Corner of the Atrium of the Altar**, arises the image of *tree with a globe in front of it that is situated at the center of a large banquet.*

In the **West of the Atrium of the Altar**, arises the image of *a man placing a sword into a burning furnace.*

In the **North Corner of the Atrium of the Altar**, arises the image of *man inside a small prison cell, standing in an empty jar.*

In the **North of the Atrium of the Altar**, arises the image of *desk, a skiff and a throne situate in a circle. At the desk sits an educated man, at the skiff, a fisherman, and at the throne, a ruler.*

In the **East Corner of the Atrium of the Basilica**, arises the image of *sheep with a cross drawn in red upon it, standing before a pool.*

In the **East of the Atrium of the Basilica**, arises the image of a *woman sitting on a stool next to a hot spring, holding a treasure chest.*

In the **South Corner of the Atrium of the Basilica**, arises the image of man in in the *desert staring in great delight at a welcoming mirage.*

In the **South of the Atrium of the Basilica**, arises the image of *man wearing a golden badge while playing a horn and standing on a platter.*

In the **West Corner of the Atrium of the Basilica**, arises the image of *ghost holding a lantern standing over a bier.*

In the **West of the Atrium of the Basilica**, arises the image of *man riding a camel, carrying a box and wearing a quiver over his shoulder.*

In the **North Corner of the Atrium of the Basilica**, arises the image of *dragon wearing a yoke and flying out of an inferno.*

In the **North of the Atrium of the Basilica**, arises the image of *the furies creating rows in the soil with a hoe and sowing seeds from a bottle into them.*

In the **East Corner of the Atrium of the Prison**, arises the image of *image of a handcuffed man being hanged with a noose and a snake beneath him.*

In the **East of the Atrium of the Prison**, arises the image of a *man with a guitar in one hand, an axe in the other, and a parrot on his shoulder.*

In the **South Corner of the Atrium of the Prison**, arises the image of *maniple crossing a bridge beneath dark clouds.*

In the **South of the Atrium of the Prison**, arises the image of *beautiful woman wearing a bracelet and playing the harp. A man stands beside her, staring at a compass.*

In the **West Corner of the Atrium of the Prison**, arises the image of *death using a cane, standing in mud.*

In the **West of the Atrium of the Prison**, arises the image of *old woman scooping frogs from the dirt.*

In the **North Corner of the Atrium of the Prison**, arises the image of *a ghoul carrying a basket and a fan.*

In the **North of the Atrium of the Prison**, arises the image of *man wearing a bearskin in the snow, studying some dung.*

In the **East Corner of the Atrium of the House**, arises the image of *pile of ash a coal and a woman using bellow upon them.*

In the **East of the Atrium of the House**, arises the image of a *man playing the flute, standing next to a pile of books.*

In the **South Corner of the Atrium of the House**, arises the image of *dog standing before a shelf with a figurine on it.*

In the **South of the Atrium of the House**, arises the image of *man wearing spurs holding a sword and dog beside him.*

In the **West Corner of the Atrium of the House**, arises the image of *cat on a platter next to a knife beside it.*

In the **West of the Atrium of the House**, arises the image of *a cat hanging from a hook over a shrine.*

In the **North Corner of the Atrium of the House**, arises the image of *a man rising out from a lagoon carrying a handful of nails and a pocket watch.*

In the **North of the Atrium of the House**, arises the image of *woman with very long hair standing before a tree with an owl in it.*

In the **East Corner of the Atrium of the Colt**, arises the image of *man with a musket, carrying a breadbasket covered in thorns.*

In the **East of the Atrium of the Colt**, arises the image of a *man covered by a linen sheet and a shield; flies swarm about.*

In the **South Corner of the Atrium of the Colt**, arises the image of *man with a knife slicing meat off of a bone.*

In the **South of the Atrium of the Colt**, arises the image of *man slamming a gavel onto a stone while holding a book.*

In the **West Corner of the Atrium of the Colt**, arises the image of *man with a handful of gems, throwing darts into a rose bush.*

In the **West of the Atrium of the Colt**, arises the image of *two men on either side of a garland, one wielding a club, the other an axe.*

In the **North Corner of the Atrium of the Colt**, arises the image of *dog wearing a muzzle trying to eat a stick of butter; a right triangle is seen on the ground.*

In the North **of the Atrium of the Colt**, arises the image of *a man holding a fork, trapped in a net with a bunch of fish.*

An actual atria

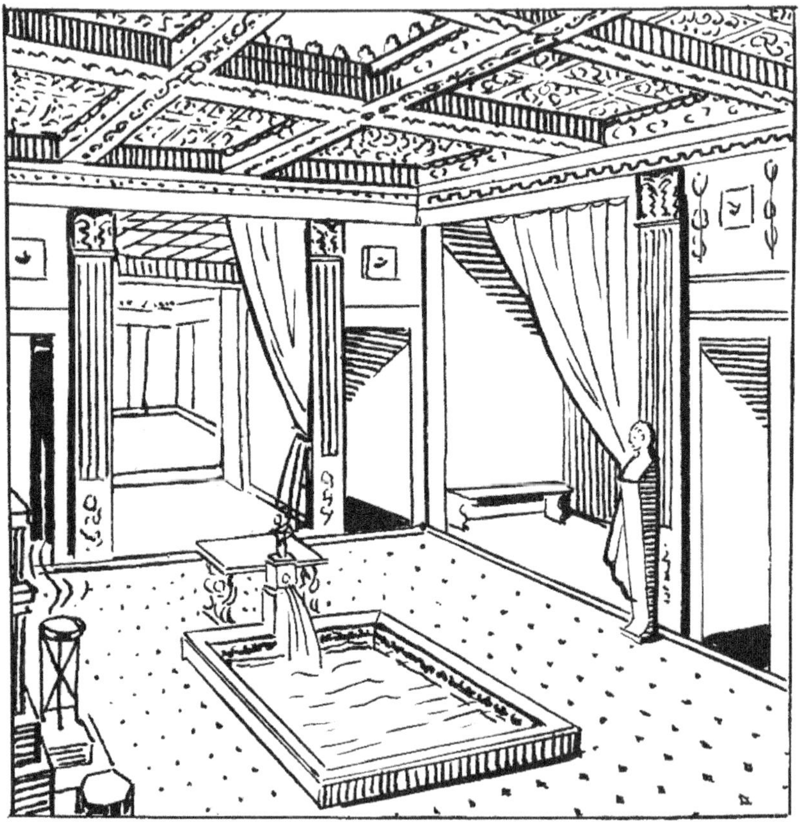

* Lawrence Alma-Tadema, *A Roman Amateur*, 1870

Part 13 | For Geography

In the same way as we applied the Two Alphabets to the creation of mnemonic imagery for the Elements of the Periodic Table, we can also apply them to the memorization of geographic elements, as for example the countries and capitals of Europe shown on the following page:

COUNTRY	CAPITAL	COUNTRY	CAPITAL
Albania	Tirana	Andorra	Andorra la Vella
Austria	Vienna	Belarus	Minsk
Belgium	Brussels	Bosnia and Herzegovina	Sarajevo
Bulgaria	Sofia	Croatia	Zagreb
Czech Republic	Prague	Denmark	Copenhagen
Estonia	Tallinn	*Faroe Islands*	Tórshavn
Finland	Helsinki	France	Paris
Germany	Berlin	Gibraltar	Gibraltar
Greece	Athens	Guernsey	Saint Peter Port
Hungary	Budapest	Iceland	Reykjavik
Ireland	Dublin	*Isle of Man*	Douglas
Italy	Rome	*Jersey*	Saint Helier
Kosovo	Pristina	Latvia	Riga
Liechtenstein	Vaduz	Lithuania	Vilnius
Luxembourg	Luxembourg	Former Yugoslav Republic of Macedonia	Skopje
Malta	Valletta	Moldova	Chisinau
Monaco	Monaco	Montenegro	Podgorica
Netherlands	Amsterdam	Norway	Oslo
Poland	Warsaw	Portugal	Lisbon
Romania	Bucharest	Russia	Moscow
San Marino	San Marino	Serbia	Belgrade
Slovakia	Bratislava	Slovenia	Ljubljana
Spain	Madrid	Sweden	Stockholm
Switzerland	Berne	Ukraine	Kiev
United Kingdom	London	Vatican City	Vatican City

Like before, these pairs will be primary symbolized by objects, which are then connected by actions to show association.

The Countries, their Capitals, and images:

Albania and Tirana | **L-B-N and TIR-N** | *A southern man drinking a libation (ice tea for example) kicking a man holding a tire iron (tir-n).*

Austria and Vienna | **AS-TREE and V-N** | *An asthmatic climbing a tree causing it to fall onto a van.*

Belgium and Brussels | **BEL-J and BRUS** | *A bellhop eating jam very sloppily with a brush.*

Bulgaria and Sofia | **BUL-G and SOFA** | *A Bull firing a gun into a sofa.*

Czech Republic and Prague | **CH-K and R-P-B-L and P-RAG** | *A man playing checkers firing red paint-balls at his opponent who is wiping his face with a purple rag.*

Estonia and Tallinn | **STON and TALL-INN** | *A man throwing stones at a tall inn.*

Finland and Helsinki | **FIN-LA and HEL-SINK** | *A whale's fin smashing into a lamp causing it to falling into the water and sink into hell.*

Germany and Berlin | **GR-MAN and B-R-L** | *A growling man in a barrel.*

Greece and Athens | **GRE and A-TH** | *An very thin ancient Greek man (wearing a toga of course).*

Hungary and Budapest | **HUNG and BUD** | *A very hungry Buddha.*

Ireland and Dublin | **I-RLD and DUBL** | *An image of yourself rolling doubles with two dice.*

Italy and Rome | **IT-Y and ROM** | *An itchy Roman soldier.*

Kosovo and Pristina | **K-O-SO and PRI** | *An Orange King kicking a soccer ball with a Priest.*

Liechtenstein and Vaduz | **LI-EN and VAD** | *Darth Vader licking the shoes of Einstein or vice versa.*

Luxembourg and Luxembourg | **LU-M-BRG** | *A man with a cross necklace carrying two maids stuffed in two bags of luggage across a bridge.*

Malta and Valletta | **M-L-T and V-L-T** | *A valet driving a car into molten lava.*

Monaco and Monaco | **M-N-C and M-N-C** | *Two monks eating tacos.*

Netherlands and Amsterdam | **N-THR-L and MS-R-DAM** | *A Neanderthal driving a red Mercedes off a dam.*

Poland and Warsaw | **POL and WAR-SAW** | *A man cutting a pole with a bloody saw.*

Romania and Bucharest | **ROMAN and BU-CH** | *A Roman Soldier fighting a meat butcher holding a cleaver.*

San Marino and San Marino | **SAN-MARE and SAN-MARE** | *Two adult female horses running through the sand on a beach.*

Slovakia and Bratislava | **SLO-V-K and B-RAT-LAVA** | *A slow Viking spearing a blue rat into lava.*

Spain and Madrid | **SPA and MA-DR** | *A can of spam being eaten by a dripping Freemason.*

Switzerland and Berne | **S-IT-RL-D and B-RN** | *A man sitting down and rolling into barn.*

United Kingdom and London | **UN-T- KING-DOM and L-N-DON** | *A king being untied from the top of a dome, falling to ground to be eaten by a Lion sitting before a Mafia Don.*

Andorra and Andorra La Vella | **AN-DO-R and AN-DO-R-LA-V** | *Two anacondas proceeding through a door. One coils around a lawyer and vomits.*

Belarus and Minsk | **BEL-RU and MI-S** | *A bellhop drinking rum while pouring milk down a sink.*

Bosnia-Herzegovina and Sarajevo | **B-S and H-R-Z-G-VIN and S-RA-EVO** | *A bus running into a man eating a heart while riding a zebra caught in a vine. Inside the bus is a sailor with a rat on his shoulder reading Darwin.*

Croatia and Zagreb | **CRO and Z-GR** | *Crows attack a zoo keeper holding grapes.*

Denmark and Copenhagen | **DE and COP-HA** | *A demon eating a cop in Hades or wearing a silly hat.*

Faroe Islands and Torshavn | **F-R and I-LA and TOR-SHA** | *a ferret landing a plane through a tornado filled with sharks.*

France and Paris | **FR and PA-R** | *A frog eating a pear.*

Gibraltar and Gibraltar | **GI-ALTAR and GI ALTAR** | *Two gypsies on an altar.*

Guernsey and Saint Peter Port | **GU-RN-EY and SAN-PE-PO** | *Many people covered in sand being carried away on gurneys.*

Iceland and Reykjavik | **ICE and R-K-VIK** | *A Viking standing on ice, holding a rake.*

Isle of Man and Douglas | **ISLE and D-GLAS** | *Many Men standing in the aisle of a church. All around them is dark glass.*

Jersey and Saint Helier | **JERSEY and SA-H-L** | *Many men wearing jerseys in a sandy hall.*

Latvia and Riga | **L-TV and R-G** | *A man spilling a latte on a beautiful rug.*

Lithuania and Vilnius | **LI-TH-N and VIL** | *A man in a limo handing a thermometer to a naked woman holding a vile of some chemical.*

Macedonia and Skopje | **MACE and SKOP** | *Ronald McDonald holding a large, scoped rifle.*

Moldova and Chisinau | **MOL-DOV and CH-SI** | *A chimpanzee doing sign language with a blond mole.*

Montenegro and Podgorica | **MON-TEN and POD-GO** | *A monkey wearing a beautiful necklace at a podium surrounded by goats.*

Norway and Oslo | **NO-WAY and O-SLO** | *"There is no way i'm going on that slope!"*

Portugal and Lisbon | **PORT-GAL and LI-S** | *A portal with a galaxy behind. A car drive through the portal and it's licence plate falls off.*

Russia and Moscow | **RUS-I and MOS-COW** | *A man is rushing to the mosque to see the cows.*

Serbia and Belgrade | **S-R-B and BEL-GR** | *A silver bee ringing a bell.*

Slovenia and Ljubljana | **SLO-V-N and L-J-B-L-J-N** | *A slowly walking viking carrying a naked woman past a log cabin with a jaguar in it and entering into a log cabin with a Judge.*

Sweden and Stockholm | **S-WED and S-OCK-HOL** | *A man covered in seaweed throwing wet socks into a hole in the beach.*

Ukraine and Kiev | **KRA and K-E** | *A giant key dangling from a crane.*

Vatican City and Vatican City | **V-T-CAN-SI and V-T-CAN-SI** | *Two vagrants standing outside a temple drinking beer from cans and then throwing them at the temple. Inside the temple stand Siamese Twins.*

The memorization of these one hundred elements and their pair relationships is by no means an easy task, but with mnemotechnics the difficulty is decreased and their memories are improved.

Similarly, these elements should perhaps be bound onto loci of some memory palace particularly designated to hold them. Indeed, it would be prudent to use a memory palace with a layout based upon the actual map of Europe, so as to show their spatial allocation.

Part 14 | Natural Symmetry

Every object or thing to be remembered has multiple categories or topics associated with it, and these are almost always *quantity, quality, substance, relation, affection, posture, state, action, time, sound, location,* (14) and *shape,* (15) Furthermore, everything participating in these categories may be subject to three divisions according to sameness or difference of terms, which are Numerical, Specific, and Generic. By *numerical* it is meant that there is more than one name for the same thing; by *specific,* that there are several things but that they do not differ in species; and by *generic* that things fall under the same genus, i.e., horse and man.(16) Now, any particular term to be memorized, in its real form, may either partake of some or all of these categories but never none. This method seeks to create MU images based off of the natures of the things to be remembered. By nature, we mean how the object is being in respect to those categories aforementioned.

For example, if we wish to create an MU for the word "war," without taking into account the sounds of the word, measuring its natures, we might say that war in substance is *death*, in activity, *destruction*, and in location, *everywhere*. Thus, our MU might be the image of a *man carrying a sickly infant* and striking a *globe* with a *bloody sword*. In this example, the sickly infant signifies death, the bloody sword, destruction, and the globe itself the idea that war is everywhere. Moreover, this method is quite aptly suited for memorizing words as they constitute parts of sentences, and when the need for variation arises in relation to the formation of MUs when using the Alphabets. Either method is suitable, but their powers are magnified if used in concert.

As an example of their combinatorial use, let us use these two methods to memorize the Spanish word for *apple*. The Spanish word for apple is *manzana*. We must note that the defining similarity between the English word *apple* and the word *manzana* is inherently what they represent, that is, a real apple. Thusly, our symbols for them – our MUs – should have something to do with the universal nature of an apple since that is what is predicated of both the words "manzana" and "apple."

To begin, let's create a table like such:

Category	(The Real Entity)	Mnemonic Images	Major Phonetic Components of New Term
Quantity			
Quality			
Substance			
Relation			
Affection			
Posture			
State			
Action			
Location			

Secondly, we should refine our categories and define the nature of the particular real entity according to them:

	Apple (English)
Appearance	Red
Location	Tree
Action	Provides sustenance

Thirdly, choose the major phonetic components that you wish to work with from the term-to-be-memorized and then use your intellect to discover visible entities which have similar natures in each category and whose first letters or syllables correspond to those sounds. Please understand, however, that the order in which the columns are filled is ultimately up to the practitioner and determined by what is practical or convenient rather than according to absolute necessity. Moreover, understand that the table is merely a visual aid and all of this may be done in the mind if you want:

	Apple (English)	Memory Images	Manzana (Spanish)
Appearance	Red	Meat	*m*
Location	Tree	Zebra striped tree	*z*
Action	Provides sustenance	Nutrients (A basket of fruit)	*n*

Finally, create the multiform image using those entities and place it in its allotted location in your memory-city: *Imagine a zebra-striped tree with meat hanging from it and a man balancing a basket of fruit on his head standing in front of the tree.*

It is improbable, I think, that you will forget such a strange and one-of-a-kind image, as it is certainly not something one sees every day, or that exists in actual reality other than now within your own imagination. This unique image will not be forgotten.

To recall this multiform image, merely observe its nature and your mind shall naturally relate it to the actual reality that its MU represents. In other words, through seeing the image you shall recall the letters and therefore the term, and by the images themselves recall the real entity.

However, the method based on nature is not always applicable because some terms do not easily lend themselves to the Topics, and these are usually more scientific terms. In those cases, it is ideal to apply the Alphabets alone. But remember that the Alphabets are predicated by the Category of Sound and therefore take advantage of Natural Symmetry, so it is completely justified to combine the two methods.

But, in relation to the particular example shown before, which concerns two terms with self-referential qualities, i.e. *apple* and *manzana*, we can merely form the MU as the image of a *man eating an apple*, and this will likely be effective in associating the Spanish term with the English one.

Part 15 | For Mathematical Equations

This technique requires the creation of particular images for each sign that may potentially arise in a mathematical equation. For example, the plus or minus sign, or the integral sign. Subsequently, through order and sequence we may create MUs which represent mathematical equations. Signs for numbers may be drawn from this table but you may also observe Part 16, "For the Memorization of Numbers" for a more specific method.

Number	Letters	Greek equivalents
0	n/a	
1	a	α (alpha)
2	b	β (beta)
3	c	κ (Kappa)
4	d	δ (Delta)
5	e	ε (Epsilon)
6	f	ϝ Digamma
7	g	γ (Gamma)
8	h	
9	i	ι (Iota)
10	j	
20	k	
30	l	λ (Lambda)
40	m	μ (Mu)
50	n	ν (Nu)
60	o	ο (Omicron)
70	p	π (Pi)
80	q	
90	r	ρ (Rho)
100	s	σ (Sigma)
200	t	τ (Tau)
300	u	υ (Upsilon)
400	v	Leftover Greek Letters: ζ, η, θ, ξ, ϟ, φ, χ, ψ, ω, ϡ
500	w	
600	x	
700	y	
800	z	

For anything higher than 10, excluding multiples of 10 and 100, an MU may be formed through the addition of letters. That is, if we desire the form and MU for the number 333, we should create a multiform image using the images for 3, 30, and 300. For numbers 900 and above, we shall use other means, such as an image for consecutivity (cc) which should itself be defined by a symbol. For example when we must illustrate a number such as 200,200, this number should be symbolized using the images for 200, 200, and cc, and through the application of proper order and sequence could be visualized as *200-cc-200*. So if we use the image of a tiger to represent the number 200, and the image of a rope to signify consecutivity, then for our conjoined MU for representing the number two hundred thousand and two hundred, we should envision the image of two tigers pulling on either end of a rope.

However, most equations do not use numbers directly, and often Greek letters are used as place holders in equations, so these have been included in the table for your convenience. We can also easily create images for Greek letters using the alphabets. For example, the MU for "alpha" – AL-FA might consist of a falcon (FA) perched on an altar (AL).

Common mathematical symbols like '*c*' for the speed of light may be given self-referential symbols, e.g., a light bulb, but specifics are left up to the individual practitioner. The leftover Greek letters, in order as they are shown in the table, are Zeta, Eta, Theta, Xi, Episemon bau, Phi, Chi, Psi, Omega, and Sanpi. All are the lowercase versions.

Some various images which may be used to represent the basic symbols of mathematics:

Sign	Images
Addition	Acts of Creativity or Showing Improvement
Subtraction	Acts of Destruction or Showing Disfigurement
Multiplication	Substances of Creation
Division	Substances of Destruction
Derivitive	Quality of Creation
Integral	Quality of Destruction
Exponent	Acts from Above
Root	Acts from Below
Parenthesis	Substances of Containment or Bounding Images
Equality	Juxtaposed Images not Causally Interacting
Delta	Triangular Forms
Decimal	Acts of Emerging
Consecutivity	Some Elongated Connection

Finally, it is definitely necessary to represent order in mathematics according to the *Order of Operations* and the actual sequence of terms within any particular equation. For example, we may want to memorize the equation $(2x + 5)^2$ and not $2x + 5^2$, which are not the same. This is a very simple example, but the principle is universal for all equations.

In order to illustrate Order of Operations we must have a way of ordering our symbols to imply the actual order of the terms in our equations. This may be accomplished using the Method of Loci and Sequence and Order.

Next are shown some examples of the creation of multiform images for equations while taking Order of Operations into account and through the application of the previously shown table:

Example 1:

$$\sigma = \sqrt{\frac{\int (X_i - \mu)^2}{N}}$$

We must first give images to our terms according to the Alphabets and the Thirty Two Methods:

σ **(sigma)** = *A SINGER BALANCING A SNAKE FROM ONE HAND TO THE OTHER, IN A BELL CURVE SHAPE, ALL WHILE BALANCING TWO DICE ON HER TONGUE*
(The snake and the two dice stand for [S]tandard [D]eviation).

(=) = JUXTAPOSED IMAGES

(√) = *A BOAR-HEADED MAN HOLDING A VAJRA*

∑ **(integral)** = *PILE OF BONES*

X = *A SHIELD-BEARING SOLDIER*

i = *AN EYE*

(−) = *BEING STABBED BY A SWORD*
μ = *A COW-HEADED WOMAN*(17)

(/) = *A LARGE TREE*

$\wedge 2 = A\ BEAR\text{-}HEADED\ MAN\ HOLDING\ A$
$SKULL\ FILLED\ WITH\ BLOOD$

$N = A\ NAKED\ WOMAN$

$(()) = A\ COFFIN$

Thusly, in the center place of some MR designated for this equation (though multiple equations can, of course, be placed in a single room if you want), place the image of a *Singer balancing a snake from one hand to the other in a bell curve shape, and balancing two dice on her tongue*. To her right, separated, envision a *large tree*. Then, to the left of the large tree, imagine a large sword and *shield-bearing soldier* with a third-*eye*. Between this soldier and the large tree place a *cow-headed woman* being *stabbed* by the soldier's sword. Have them both, together, standing in a *coffin* located in a *pile of bones*. Next, imagine a *bear-headed man holding a skull filled with blood* standing to the right of the coffin with one foot resting on the coffins edge. To the left of the coffin standing in the pile of bones, imagine the image of a *boar headed man holding a vajra*. Next, imagine a *naked woman* standing to the right of the large tree also with a boar-headed man with a vajra standing next to her. Now we should apply action and reaction in order to improve the memory of this image.

This equation is for the discovery of the standard deviation and is a formula commonly found in many statistics textbooks. It will likely be encountered in any college level statistics course.

Example 2:

$$E = mc^2$$

The Images:

E = *AN EAGLE*

(=) = JUXTAPOSED IMAGES

m = *MIRROR*

(*) = *APHRODITE*

c = *A CANDLE*

^2 = *BOAR HEADED MAN HOLDING A PAINTBRUSH*

Thus, imagine an *eagle circling from above*. Below it, imagine the image of *Aphrodite* holding a *candle* in her left hand and a *mirror* in her right. To her left, imagine the image of *boar headed man holding a paintbrush* and painting the light bulb black.

Part 16 | For the Memorization of Numbers

For the memorization of numbers, while the MU method is truly functional and works, there is another method which the practitioner must be aware, and this is the method whereby words are formed to represent numbers and fractions by drawing forth their vowel and consonantal equivalents from a table. Now, this is a very old mnemonic technique and we quote from an old source to illustrate this method for memorizing numbers: *"The principal Part of this Method is briefly this; To remember in History Chronology, Geography, etc., a Word is formed, the Beginning whereof being the first Syllable or Syllables of the Thin sought, does, by frequent Repetition, of course draw after it the latter Part, which is so contrived as to five the Answer. Thus, in History, the Deluge happened in the Year before Christ two Thousand three Hundred forth eight; this is signified by the Word Deletok: Del standing for the DELUGE, and etok for 2348. In Astronomy, the Diameter of the Sun (SOLIS Diameter) is eight Hundred twenty two Thousand one Hundred and forty eight English Miles; this is signified by Soldi-ked-afei, Soldi standing for Diameter of the Sun, ked-afei for 822,148; and so of the rest, as will be shown more fully in the proper Place. How these Words come to signify these Things, or contribute to the Remembering of them is now to be shown. The first thing to be done is to learn exactly the following Series of Vowels and*

Consonants which are to represent the numerical Figures, so as to be able, at Pleasure to form a Technical Word, which shall stand for any Number, or to resolve a Word already formed into the Number which it stands for.

Number	Vowel	Consonant
1	a	b
2	e	d
3	i	t
4	o	f
5	u	l
6	au	s
7	oi	p
8	ei	k
9	ou	n
0	y, w	z

"The first five Vowels in order naturally represent 1, 2, 3, 4, 5. The Diphthong au, being composed of a 1 and u 5 stands for 6; oi for 7, being composed of o 4 and i 3; ou for 9 being composed of o 4 and u 5. The Diphthong ei will easily be remembered for eight, being the Initials of the Word. In likes Manner for the Consonants, where the Initials could conveniently be retained, they are made use of to signify the Number, as t for three, f for four, s for six and n for nine. The rest were assigned without any particular Reason, unless possibly p may be more easily remembered for 7 or Septem, k for 8 or όKτό, d for 2 or duo, b for 1 as being the first Consonant, and l for 5, being the Roman Letter for 50[…]."

On division from the same source: "*[Similarly]* it will sometimes also of Use to be able to set down a Fraction, *which may be done in the following Manner: Let r be the Separatrix between the Numerator and the Denominator, the first coming before, the other after it."*(18)

We shall similarly signify the decimal point by the consonantal letter *m*.

Our own syllabic and single letters alphabets for MU creation are sufficient for the memorization of the terms, but for the memorization of numbers, this method is perhaps superior, although both work. Let us apply this method to the memorization of the Element Beryllium and its Atomic Mass: Thus our MU for Beryllium is the image of a 'beautiful woman taking a bath, pouring water on herself from a large barrel.' The significant term being 'Barrel.' The Atomic Mass of Beryllium is 9.012182. Therefore, according to the table, our name for Beryllium's Atomic Mass is oum-wat-ake (9-012-182). Combing the two terms we then have: *Barrel-oumwatake*. Oumwatake can be further developed into a visual MU itself using the two Alphabets and then bound onto the image of the barrel in the MU for the Element Beryllium if the practitioner prefers. Or, merely associate the sound "oumwatake" with the image of the Barrel and leave it at that if the practitioner deems such to be sufficient for memory.

Part 17 | For the Memorization of Poetry, Sentences, and Paragraphs

In general, for the memorization of any set of words, the methods shown in Part 12 of this book are applicable. But to increase specificity on this topic I shall quote from another old mnemonic work from a chapter titled 'Poetry and Prose:' *In order to commit to memory any particular piece of poetry which may be divided into stanzas, each consisting of four, six, eight, or ten lines, etc. it is necessary to take one stanza at a time, to read it over and to select the principal objects or images, and combine them with the first [background(19)]; attach the next stanza to the second [background], and so on with the remaining stanzas. By these means we are not only enabled to recite the whole poem in regular order, but to repeat any one or more stanzas in any order, – to determine the numerical situation of any line or word in the poem – and to say how often any particular word may occur. As we are able to repeat any stanza in the poem, it will only be needful to count the lines or words, if it be required to determine the numerical situation of any line or word. It will not be difficult to apply these principles to the repetition of poetry. A single illustration, perhaps, will be sufficient... We shall five the following [example] from Nolegar, as quoted by Feyjoo, in his Cartas Erutitas,*(20)

"*Denix Divina*
"*De tan bellas alas*
"*Humilde, y piudisa*
"*Al Ciclo te ensalzas*

"*Divine Phoenix,*"
"*With such beautiful wings,*"
"*Humble and Merciful,*"
"*Thou raisest to Heaven.*"

The Phoenix in the first verse of this stanza (says Nolegar) must be placed [on the background or the wall of the first room] on the right hand, and a Papal Crown, or Tiara, or any other thing belonging to the Church, must be put on its head; because we cannot apply any other material object, to represent the Word Divine; we may then make a reflection or two on these images, and say, why has a Phoenix, the Papal Crown on its head? It is a Divine Phoenix… Then the second [background or the wall of the first room] shall be taken for the second verse, and a drum with a stick to beat it, may be placed there. The stick, [drum, and drummer] may explain the word [de]… I would put two beautiful woman sitting by the drummer, who should have two wings lying at his feet; and speaking of the second [background or wall of the first room] De tan bellas alas (with such beautiful wings)…" (21)

Thusly, each of the lines of the stanza may be written upon a background of some MR through the placement of their MUs through Natural and Phonetic Symmetry, or upon the same background when that is more convenient. This is the method whereby we may bind any string of words unto memory with great permanence; this technique is not restricted to poetry, but may likewise be applied to the memorization of definitions, facts, and small quotes, etc.

Part 18 | The Method of Loci Applied to Poetry, Sentences, and Paragraphs

A very powerful form of memory field may be created through the application of the Method of Loci to poetry, sentences, and paragraphs. In this technique, those various bodies of words themselves are turned into memory fields. Each and every word potentially, including prepositions, conjunctions, pronouns, etc., is memorized through MU generation and linking as shown in the previous chapter, but instead of placing each of the MUs into a separate memory field, the MUs are angulated according to the actual visual appearance of the body of words. For example, a single stanza of a poem might be considered a single MR, and an entire poem an MRS. Any poetry book could therefore be considered as a readily available MRS^2. Furthermore, this technique is especially applicable to poetry, for poems are often succinctly brief and contain grand imagery; likewise for many religious texts as, for example, the Bible's *Revelations* comes to mind.

Part 19 | Paintings and 2-Dimensionality

An interesting feature of memory is that two dimensional pictures welcome themselves easily to being remembered, perhaps even more so than three dimensional forms, especially within the borders of a beautiful frame. This, I believe, is because the mind finds it easier to cognize two-dimensional forms as opposed to those of three dimensions or higher, which may be more taxing. Furthermore, the frames of a painting lend themselves nicely to categorization, which is pivotal for memorization. And, as we have all experienced, a nice frame can improve the perceived quality of a painting, making it both more memorable and striking. Paintings within frames can also be easily broken up into different loci. We can even commission the painting of our MUs and place them in our actual homes.

Therefore, at times you may instead bind your MUs and MRs into canvases and frames and then place these upon your backgrounds in your memory-cities. As well, you may place the images of entire MRSs and memory-cities into frames, and thusly enable yourself to store a great number of these in sequence in some MR designated for them. That is, paintings are aptly suited to becoming MRs and MRSs themselves. This is demonstrated in the following painting(s) by *Giovanni Paolo Pannini*. The painting by *Albrecht* is representative of how this technique may be applied to MUs within paintings; Albrecht's *Dürer Melencolia* is a perfect example of how a painting can become a highly symbolic, geometrically oriented MR.

Giovanni Paolo Pannini, Gallery of Views of Ancient Rome, 1758

Albrecht, Dürer Melencolia I, 1514

Part 20 | On Sexualization

The sexualization of MUs is a very important topic, as this technique will greatly improve the ease of which an image shall be remembered, for the emotions, feelings, and sensations associated with sex, being invigorated through concentration, can powerfully bind images into memory; but why is this? Perhaps because sex and the organs of reproduction, including the breasts which a baby is drawn to for nutrients and health, is of the utmost importance to the survival of humans and therefore is naturally hardwired into the functions of the brain. Binding sexualized images to the memory naturally associates them with the neural-nexus associated with sex and survival. Again, like with our sense of space and the Method of Loci, would it not be reasonable to adapt the sexual faculty to improving our memories?

In this technique, we should attempt to make our MUs sexual by having them, if they are female in some way, showing a breast or more. Likewise, with your imagination, you may create MUs of even greater sexual affect when you see fit to do so. Images of both sexes may be used of course, according to necessity. A quote from this method's progenitor on this matter: "*I usually fill my memory-places with the images of beautiful women, which excite my memory . . . and believe me when I use beautiful woman as memory images, I find it much easier to arrange and repeat the notions which I have entrusted*

[handwritten notes: Makes sense! Likely more efficient than trying to force and visualise emotional reactions. — Statues — People — Nudity — Art — Sexuality]

to those places. You now have a most useful secret of artificial memory, a secret which I have (through modesty) long remained silent about: if you want to remember quickly, dispose the images of the most beautiful virgins into memory places; the memory is marvelously excited by images of woman . . . This precept is useless to those who dislike woman and they will find it very difficult to gather the fruits of this art. I hope chaste and religious men will pardon me: I cannot pass over in silence a rule which has earned me much praise and honor on account of my abilities in the art, because I wish, with all my heart, to leave excellent successors behind me." – Peter of Ravenna(22)

138

139

*1) Roman marble statue of wounded Amazon from the 1st or 2nd century
*2) Roman copy of Leochares' Belvedere Apollo 130 – 140AD after a Greek bronze original of 330 – 320 BC

*The Three Graces

*3 Images statues from Khajuraho Temple Complex

143

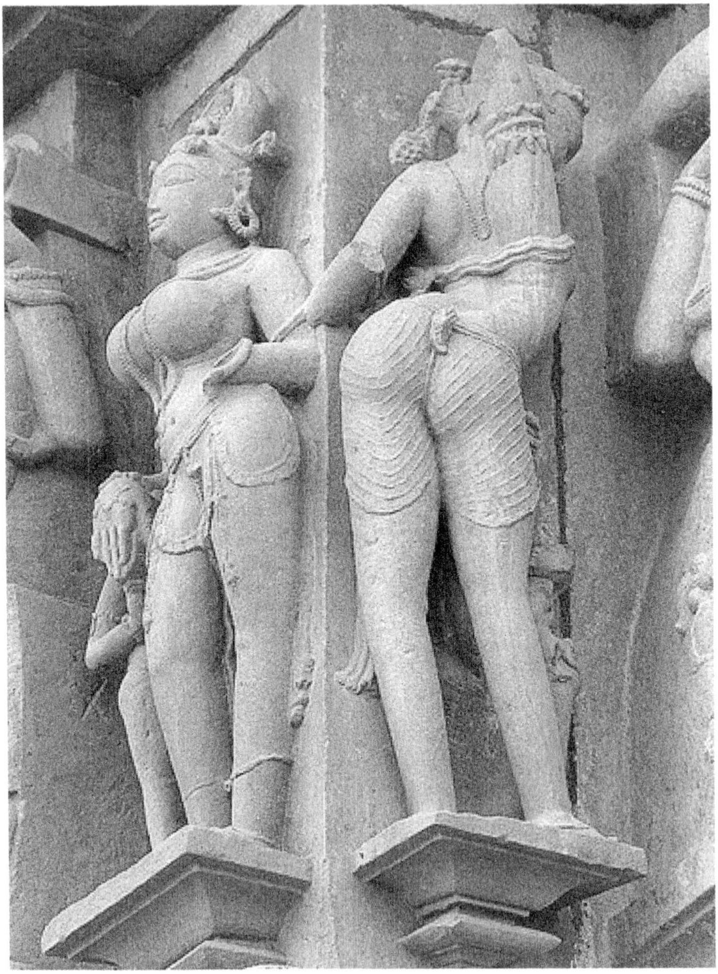

*Ancient Hindu painting containing a great variety of highly sexualized symbolic imagery.

There will not be provided a section on the opposite of this which is torture, and therefore pain and fear, which are also powerful at binding images into memory – again, because of the association with survival. I think it will be easy to infer the how-to of such a technique. But, also, things which are feared, hated, or loved are also powerful binding tools, and the practitioner should keep this in mind when creating MUs.

Part 21 | Temporal Mnemonics and Temporal Loci: How to Memorize Times, Dates, and Facts in History

First, let us define the concepts of *Mnemonic Order* and *Mnemonic Sequence*: a Mnemonic Order is the arrangement of MUs in space and Mnemonic Sequence is the arrangement of MUs in time. The question then arises: Is it possible to have a sequence of MUs without also having their order in space? Of course, and this arrangement is accomplished through linking normally, whereas arrangement in space is accomplished through angulation.

Temporal Mnemonics, therefore, regards the application of the human sense of time, as opposed to the application of the sense of space in the Method of Loci, to the creation of MLs. However a distinction needs to be made between a *Spatial Memory Location* and a *Temporal Memory Location* (tML). A Spatial Memory Location is a "place," an object, or a corner in a room, etc. So, then, to the mind, what is a "place" in time? Well, places in space are defined by magnitudes, distances, dimensions, feet, meters, angles, etc, so it seems reasonable to assume that places in time are things like seconds, minutes, hours, days, weeks, months, and years, etc, for that is how we measure time. In other words, our Temporal Memory Locations are increments, or magnitudes of time, and those that we are most familiar with are *seconds*, *minutes*, *hours*, *days*, *weeks*, *months*, and *years*, etc. This leads us to the *Complex Method* for memorizing time relevant information, such as times, dates, and facts in history.

The Complex Method:

Getting to the point, the Complex Method involves the angulation of *Temporal Memory Fields* (tMFs) which are series of temporally angulated MUs having the forms of our seconds, minutes, hours, days, weeks, months, and years, etc. This creates a conjunct memory field which is "simultaneously" both spatial and temporal; that is, perhaps, a "spatiotemporal" memory field. This conjunct will be termed as a *Complex Memory Field* of the *First Order* (cMF^1), implying that the field consists of two spectrums of sensory information. In this case, space and time. Likewise, a *Second Order* Complex Memory Field would imply three types of spectral sensory information, and so on and so forth to the *nth* number of senses.

The first step in forming a Temporal Memory Field is to associate with some MU a *length of time*, that is, a tML. This is analogous to the angulation of an MU with an ML; the MU becomes the particular length of time – a *Temporal Memory Background*. In the Complex Method we merge Temporal Memory Backgrounds with Spatial Memory Backgrounds. In other words, for example, a place in some order of objects in a MR becomes known not only by a location relative to other locations, but also by a "location in time" relative to other locations in time. Specifically, we are referring to the dates of a calendar; and for our purposes, this will be the Gregorian calendar.

The *First Step* in this process is to form an mMRS containing twelve MRSs, each with four MRs. Further, each MR should contain about seven MLs.

The *Second Step* involves associating with each of the MFs a particular tMF. For the MRSs those would be the months of the Gregorian calendar. For example, our first MRS would represent the month of January, our second MRS, February, and so on and so forth. Likewise, each MR would represent a particular week and each ML, within each MR, a particular day. Extra days must be placed about the MRs, or MRSs, somewhere determined by the practitioner. Please note the utility of the ancient Egyptian Coptic calendar in regard to the extra days: In that calendar, the year was broken up into three hundred and sixty days, twelve months based upon the Zodiac, thirty six Decans of ten days each, and five days of holidays at the end of the year. Such would likely have been the temporal foundation for the zodiacal mnemonic system of *Metrodorus of Scepsis*.

In the *Third Step* we link our MUs for the various important facts and things we want to remember in time to our particular cMLs in our now cmMRS. However, note that we must still signify in MU form the particular year of the thing in time because we do not do so in our cmMRS.

For example, if want to memorize the inauguration date of the first President of the United States, George Washington, we would first, as usual, form an MU to represent his name. This might be for the name "George," a *geode*, and for "Washington," a *washing machine*. Subsequently we form the image of a *woman placing a geode into a washing machine causing it to break*. This is our MU for the name "George Washington." Likewise, using the table from Part 16, the number of the relevant year, which is 1789, becomes *boi-kou*. Thusly, we might imagine the image of a *mischievous boy, holding a coke, placing a geode into a washing machine causing it to break* to represent the year and the substance of the particular fact. Then, because the particular days are already signified in the cmMRS, we link this MU to the particular background of February 4th, the specific day of George Washington's inauguration. In returning to that cML, we may subsequently recall the particular date, the individual, and the event.

Such suffices for an explanation of the Complex Method. However, note that a single MRS would also be sufficient if you cannot find three hundred and sixty five backgrounds to populate an mMRS. All this would mean is that you would now need to use the table from part fifteen to form two MUs for both the year and the month instead of only for the year. Such an MRS would require thirty one MLs in order to account for the maximum number of days in month.

Lastly, the reason this method is so effective is because it allows us to apply our sense of time as well as our sense of space, therefore improving the strength of the memory.

The Simple Method:

In the *Simple Method*, instead of forming a distinct memory field specifically to represent the calendar year, we instead use already formed ones. In the case of a list of the inauguration dates for United States Presidents, we would require a memory field with at least forty four continuous MLs, given that there were forty four United States Presidents (Glover Cleveland was elected twice). For example, forty four MLs from your house-MRS.

The Simple Method for memorizing such lists of dates requires only the Method of Loci and Linking. It does not require any temporal memory fields. In this method, like the complex one, we first need to understand that each date generally contains three pieces of information that need be remembered: Months, Days, and Years. In the Complex Method, potentially two of these years and months were determined by the layout of the cmMRS or cMRS, but in the simple method we do not assign temporal loci to particular locations. Instead, we memorize in MU form all of the information to be remembered. In the case of a fact like "George Washington's Birthdate," this would be the (1) *year*, 1789, the (2) *month*, February, the (3) *day*, the 4th, his (4) *name*, George Washington, and the (5) *event*, birthday. Thus, there are five pieces of distinct information that we need to convert to MUs and be able to recall, instead of three with the Complex Method. You might think this is not a big difference, but when you have to memorize hundreds, if not thousands, of particular dates, this difference becomes significant.

On the other hand, the Simple Method is perhaps preferred when your dates are less random, as for example, the inauguration dates of United States

Presidents, but because it does not use temporal loci and because the simple method requires more MUs, recollection of the memory will be more difficult.

Key Terms:

Mnemonic Order: *An arrangement of MUs in Space. Mnemonic Order is created to the Angulation of MUs.*

Mnemonic Sequence: *An arrangement of MUs in Time. Mnemonic Sequence is created through linking.*

Temporal Memory Field (tMF): *A mnemonic area consisting of a set of one or more tMLs, and possibly tMRs, tMRSs, or tmMRSs.*

Temporal Memory Location (tML): *A single "location" upon which an MU may be bound, as for example, an hour or a day. Likewise, it is possible to infer the existence of tMRs, tMRSs, and tmMRSs, and these might be greater spans of time, for example, weeks, months, and years, respectively. Although what constitutes an angle, a corner, or a wall in time remains to be determined. We do know however that our sense of time is a powerful mnemonic tool when applied to MUs.*

Complex Memory Field (cMF): *The conjunct memory field is usually comprised of a temporal memory location and a spatial one. In a spatiotemporal Complex Memory Field, tMFs become associated with sMFs such that a place, as for example, a corner in a room, becomes known by a time, a "date in time,", and the tML, likewise, by the sML. Note, however, that cMFs are not necessary composed of only sMFs with tMFs, but may also become composed of any sort of spectrum of* *sensory information, for example, the spectrum of visible light in color or a "spectrum of smells," etc.*

nth Order Complex Memory Field (cMF^n): *a MF composed of an nth number of sensory spectrums. For example, a cMF composed of three spectrums of sensory information would be a Complex Memory Field of the Second Order.*

Part 22 | On detail and Imagination

Most of all, when in the process of forming images, we must very carefully pay attention to the details. Observations such as hand placement, shirt wrinkles, posture of images, etc., shall greatly improve the ease of recognition of MUs. Actually, the act of drawing forth an image's finer points is very easy and requires merely that we know the right questions to ask of it; generally there are a finite number of questions to ask of any subject, and these are for the most part according to the Aristotelian Categories, which are reiterated here. The questions are as follows:

Substance – What is its essence? For example, is it a man, or a horse, or perhaps a house?
Quantity – How much or how many? How large?
Quality – What is its appearance? Rough? Smooth? White?
Relation – For example, is it half or perhaps a third in size relative to another?
Place – What location? Perhaps to the east? Is it within or is it outside? Is it in the first place of the first building?
Time – When is it? For example, what day is the memory? What hour? How long ago?
Posture/Position – E.g., is it sitting? What attitude?
State/Condition – How circumstanced? For example, is it armed?
Action – What is it doing? How is it active, how passive?
Affection – What is happening to it? What is it suffering?

It is suggested that in the formation and the passing through of your memory-city to ask of every image these ten questions, and in doing so you will find that the image becomes more real and more permanent in the mind.

Furthermore, in concordance with these questions we can come to understand any MU completely. However, it must be noted that these questions are merely the beginning of this science of questioning, which can become very complicated and even more useful through combination and other applications of its mystery which are, for our purposes, adequately described in this quote by Ramon Llull: *"For the purposes of reciting long passages from memory, I decided to establish some relative terms with which one could give answers concerning all things… These in fact are the terms mentioned above: 'what,' 'why,' 'how much,' and 'how.' By any one of these you will be able to repeat from memory twenty counter-arguments or whatever facts might have come to you while you were talking, and how admirable it is that you might be able to keep in mind a hundred arguments so that, as the occasion arises, you can recite them well."*(23)

Part 23 | Memory Weight

An interesting trick to solidifying an MU into memory is to imagine it to have a very great weight or a very light weight such that the image, though massive in size, is as light as a feather or that a small feather is as heavy as a mountain. In this method you should visualize yourself attempting to push the MU; imagine the object being either unmovable or very easily moved as you see fit. For some reason, this strengthens the image in the mind. So, mentally push upon your MUs and imagine them to not budge no matter what strength you apply.

Part 24 | Size Optimization

Now, this is a very important rule for memorization and forming MUs: One must never create an image that is either too large or too small, for in doing so you shall lessen the power of the image in memory. We should therefore aim to optimize the size of an image such that it is easily cognizable; the perfect size will perhaps vary for each individual practitioner of the Art of Memory, but as a general rule, make sure the image fits within the view of your mental vision. You should, that is, leave some amount of space surrounding your MUs so that you can simultaneously understand in which location it is bound up as well as its total appearance.

Part 25 | Length, Breadth, and Width Specification

Another way to improve the memorability of an image is, when in the act of creating the image, to define its dimensions: its length, breadth, width, its time of creation, and, if applicable, its age. In doing so you may easily add to the lastingness of the image in memory. For example, if your MU is of a tree and an old man, you may think to yourself about their actual height and visualize this as well as their other dimensions, including the seeming age of the man. Measure the various parts of them. For example, height and branch length and so on and so forth for every component of your MUs, MRs, MRSs, and mMRSs; and attempt to deeply relate these dimensions to one another, for dimensionality is relative and, so, without comparison, lacks reality in both the physical and mental realms.

Part 26 | Perspective Disjunction

This is a very useful technique and works through the creation of an image of your own self within your memory-city. Then, by observing yourself interacting with the various MUs and locations in the third person, and through applying the other techniques of visualization in conjunction with this, you will improve your ability to remember the MUs. You may, for example, envision yourself going up to an MU, observing it, feeling its texture, speaking to it, and generally interacting with it. This technique can add a more human and personal quality to your MUs, as well as cement them more permanently into memory.

Part 27 | Ocular Fixation

As in meditation, where one is taught to focus the inner vision at the center of the brow, likewise in envisioning our MUs we must keep them in the center of our vision, carefully focus on them, and meditate upon them. It is best that every night before bed you traverse your memory-city and observe each of your MUs both separately and in combination with each other.

Part 28 | Image Specification

It is especially important to pay attention to the several categories and questions previously mentioned. In doing so one may greatly help the binding of images into memory; this method takes advantage of the power of understanding, for by understanding we may know or remember more easily. Ask yourself this question: Will I be able to remember fuzzy, ambiguous, and incoherent images more than detailed ones, whose parts are completely known?

Part 29 | Localization and Delocalization

This technique works by visualizing the shrinking and or expanding of an MU to the point that the image becomes incomprehensible. You will notice that after a certain amount of expanding or shrinking, the MU will become delocalized; the MU will become an incorporeal idea and not an image at all. Subsequently, if you have expanded the image to the point of delocalization, shrink the image back into existence; localize it. Repeating this process of delocalization and localization will help cement the image into memory. This is similar to the act of repeating a word in order to remember it, as this technique forces re-cognition of the image over and over again.

Part 30 | Direct and Indirect Symbolism

This technique is very easy to use; we merely need to observe the secondary symbolism of an MU, that is, the symbolism which does not pertain directly to the terminology which was the cause of the creation of the MU. For example, in our multiform image for the parts of a cell, our secondary symbolism might be as such for just the images of the Usher, Throne, and Wreath: the Usher could be understood as the symbol for the Workingman, a Servant, or Nurturer. The Throne may symbolize Ruling; and the Wreath may symbolize Nature. In this way we see this MU as symbolizing the philosophical idea that the Servant is the true Ruler of Nature, and that he who provides for and nurtures others is truly the king of the world. Of course, this symbolism was not intended, for this is a symbol for the term *Eukaryote*, but by observing the MU in a different light it can become philosophically powerful, and consequently its memorability will improve. Furthermore, this technique may be spatially extended to include all the potential MUs of your greater multiform image to create a great landscape of secondary meaning.

Part 31 | Relative Orientation

For each MU, pay heed to its relative location, such as their angles and the ways they are facing. For example, you should visually observe that one image's face in one room is juxtaposed ninety degrees to another image in another room, to other images and backgrounds in its own room, for there is great power in angularity for determining which memory object is in which location.

Part 32 | Regarding Artificial Memory Cities

In substance, the artificial memory-city, its memory rooms and locations, are practically incomparable to a memory-city produced from real locations, but necessarily we must pay heed to the utility of the non-artificial memory-city regarding why it is so useful and how it comes to be so effective. Now, what is distinctive about a location in a room devoid of objects, i.e., a corner, wall, ceiling, or floor? The answer is "barely anything." The geometry of a place is somewhat variable and the relative nature of one corner compared to another is as well, but does that constitute enough distinctiveness in memory to be useful by itself? Perhaps for some but it is likely, I think, that most will find it difficult to discern one location from another and subsequently become discombobulated as they search throughout the city for that specific location, lost in the similarity of the various places. In other words, as we discussed earlier, variability is extremely important to memory. So how can we provide variability to artificial buildings, rooms, and corners, etc? Ask yourself this question: are the corners, walls, and floors of the room I am currently in occupied by objects of variable nature? Was my bedroom as a child, its various locations, filled with all sorts of different objects and things? How about my office, or my local library? Is not a room, its essence in fact, defined according to the forms and functions of the things contained therein? Therefore, it is suggested that locations be not merely known by their geometry, but by the objects, colors, and all other appearances which consistently occupy them, such that these become the locations and the locations become these.

Now, given this observation in our artificial memory-cities, systems, and rooms, we must therefore associate their MLs and general forms with certain images of differing natures, so as to make each location distinctive for the sake of the intellect's searching faculty; and these images are generally referred to as *Backgrounds*. Instead of knowing each artificial location merely by its geometry, we know them by their associated image such that the image is the ML, MR, or the MRS. For example, one background might consist of the image of a dragon, another a fountain, another a cannon, another a beach, another a banquet, and so on and so forth when the need for categorization and, therefore, distinctiveness arises.

Subsequently, in binding MUs to these backgrounds we do not merely place them in one location or another, at one corner or another, but actually bind them to the background which is already thereupon bound and memorable. Another way of putting this is that the MUs become mnemonically associated with already memorized, distinctive locations. This is extremely advantageous to memory and is partly what makes the artificial memory-city superior compared to one which consists of a real city, for one is filled with real and sometimes boring, un-strange objects, whereas the other, the artificial, can be filled with ludicrous and exceptional images which, as we know, are more conducive to memorization and recollection. Another significant difference lies in the fact that memory-cities based off of the Real are often filled with what I term as "non-sense locations." In other words, they are filled with locations which are not exactly mnemonically important, whereas, in artificial memory-cities, every location can be mnemonically relevant, and are almost always immediately juxtaposed to other mnemonically relevant locations; locations that we intend to bind MUs onto and whose backgrounds are therefore significant. An example of a non-sense location might be some random building in your home town-based memory-city, one you never visit, rarely see, and with a boring appearance. However, for these added benefits there is a cost, which is that the backgrounds in the artificial memory-city must be pre-memorized or associated with their allotted locations before new MUs can be bound to them.

As for the benefits of memory-cities based off of real, existing locations, the most significant incentive in choosing this type is that you can actually visit your memory locations in real life; in this way, there really isn't any meaningful distinction between the real and mnemonic.

I will deal entirely with the subject of artificial memory-cities in future books, providing complete examples of them for actual use by the practitioner, so understand this current book as an exposition of the general tools of this art.

Finally, in parting, let us conclude with a quote from Cicero on industry, art, and mnemonics: *"In every discipline artistic theory is of little avail without unremitting exercise, but especially in mnemonics theory is almost valueless unless made good by industry, devotion, toil, and care. You can make sure that you have as many backgrounds as possible and that these conform as much as possible to the rules; in placing the images you should exercise every day. While an engrossing preoccupation may even distract us from our other pursuits, from this activity nothing whatever can divert us. Indeed there is never a moment when we do not wish to commit something to memory, and we wish it most of all when our attention is held by business of special importance. So, since a ready memory is a useful thing, you can see clearly with what great pains we must strive to acquire so useful a faculty…"*(24)

Key Terms:

Background: *An angulated MU having been spatially integrated into a particular memory field; a visually distinct memory field whereupon other MUs may be linked, as for example, an altar, a fountain, a garden, or a person.*

Final Note

Dear Reader,

    Please let this book suffice as a guide to the creation of your own memory images, palaces, and cities, and as a self-sufficient text for the improvement of memory, but future works will go into detail about specific artificial memory-cities. Ideally one city will be covered per book, although these may eventually be consolidated into a single text. If you have found my efforts in this art to be of use to you, I hope that you can share this knowledge with your peers in the hope that they may benefit from these techniques as well.

Sincerely,
M.A. Kohain

Glossary of Terms

Angulation: *That act of transforming an MU into an ML through envisioning its specific angularity relative to other memory fields including other singular MLs.*

Background: *An angulated MU having been spatially integrated into a particular memory field; a visually distinct memory field whereupon other MUs may be linked, as for example, an altar, a fountain, a garden, or a person.*

Linking: *The process of creating a causal relation between two MUs, two MLs, or an MU and an ML, as for example, when we imagine one MU interacting physically or intentionally sharing a similar property with another MU. Furthermore, the actual link formed, the relationship between the MUs and MLs, is known as a "linkage."*

Massive Memory Room System (mMRS): *Any MRS composed of multiple MRSs. The "level" of MRS is denoted by an exponent to the right of the term.*

Memory Field: *A mnemonic area consisting of a set of one or more MLs, MRs, MRSs, or mMRSs.*

Memory Location (ML): *A single location upon which an MU may be bound, as for example, a corner in a room, a piece of furniture, a window, a doorway, an external feature to some building, or any other distinct object or unified set of objects (Note that MUs, when other MUs are bound to them, are essentially the same as MLs).*

Memory Room (MR): *A set of MLs confined in some kind of distinct, compartmentalized area, as for example, a walled room, a small garden, or a car.*

Memory Room System (MRS): *A set of MRs usually sequential in order.*

Method of Loci (or Loci Method): *The Mnemonic Device that takes advantage of the human sense of space. In this technique, symbolic images, or "MUs (Mnemonic Units)," are bound to spatially distinct and sequentially ordered mental locations called MLs (Memory Locations).*

Mnemonic Journey: *A series of mnemonic jumps; a series of cognitive movements of recollection through a set of MUs and or MLs.*

Mnemonic Jump: *The cognitive movement of recollection from one MU or ML to another.*

Mnemonic Movement: *A movement from one ML or MU to another through its linkage. Both mnemonic jumps and mnemonic journeys are mnemonic movement.*

Mnemonic Order: *An arrangement of MUs in Space. Mnemonic Order is created to the Angulation of MUs.*

Mnemonic Unit (MU): *A single instance of the application of a mnemonic device, a symbol. As for example, an apple when it symbolizes the letter 'A.'*

Mnemonic Unit Component (MUC): *A component of an MU. An MUC can also show secondary symbolism, referencing or sharing a property of another MU.*

Mnemonic Unit Nexus (MUN): *The term given to the more general or more universal MU relative to less general MUs, as for example, a MUN might be the MU formed to represent a single chapter heading in a book, a title of some list of things, or, for example, the MU for the term Eukaryotic cell, but only in so far as they are relative to sub-categorical MUs.*

Mnemonic Sequence: *An arrangement of MUs in Time. Mnemonic Sequence is created through linking.*

Mnemograph: *A detailed illustration of a memory field, showing all MRs, MRSs, and mMRSs, as well as depicting and describing all MLs and potentially all MUs bound therein and their arrangements. Essentially, a memory field blueprint.*

Complex Memory Field (cMF): *The conjunct memory field is usually comprised of a temporal memory location and a spatial one. In a spatiotemporal Complex Memory Field, tMFs become associated with sMFs such that a place, as for example, a corner in a room, becomes known by a time, a "date in time,", and the tML, likewise, by the sML. Note, however, that cMFs are not necessary composed of only sMFs with tMFs, but may also become composed of any sort of spectrum of sensory information, for example, the spectrum of visible light in color or a "spectrum of smells," etc.*

***nth* Order Complex Memory Field:** *a MF composed of an nth number of sensory spectrums. For example, a cMF composed of three spectrums of sensory information would be a Complex Memory Field of the Second Order.*

Temporal Memory Field (tMF): *A mnemonic area consisting of a set of one or more tMLs, and possibly tMRs, tMRSs, or tmMRSs.*

Temporal Memory Location (tML): *A single "location" upon which an MU may be bound, as for example, an hour or a day. Likewise, it is possible to infer the existence of tMRs, tMRSs, and tmMRSs, and these might be greater spans of time, for example, weeks, months, and years, respectively. Although what constitutes an angle, a corner, or a wall in time remains to be determined. We do know however that our sense of time is a powerful mnemonic tool when applied to MUs.*

Bibliography & Footnotes

(1) Bruno, Giordano. *On the Composition of Images, Signs & Ideas*, 1591. Trans. Charles Doria. New York: Willis, Locker & Owens, 1991. Print. ISBN 0-930279-18-2

(2) The expression "In the first place" is actually a mnemonic device referencing the Method of Loci which we will go into detail about later in the book.

(3) Michel de Montaigne, Essais, trans. M.A. Screech, The Essays of Michel de Montaigne (Harmondsworth: Allen Lane, Penguin Press, 1991), I, 9, p. 32 and II, 10, p.457 | From Rossi, Paolo. *Logic and the Art of Memory: The Quest for a Universal Language*. Trans. Clucas, Stephen Chicago: The Athlone Press and the University of Chicago, 2000. Print. Pg 3. ISBN 0-226-72826-9

(4) http://classics.mit.edu/Aristotle/memory.html | On Memory and Reminiscence. By Aristotle
Written 350 B.C.E. Translated by J. I. Beare

(5) Cicero. *Rhetorica ad Herennium*. Trans. Caplan, Harry. London, England. Harvard University Press. 1954. Print. ISBN 978-0-674-99444-7 Pg 223

(6) The letter Y could as well be substituted here.

(7) Cicero. *Rhetorica ad Herennium*. Trans. Caplan, Harry. London, England. Harvard University Press. 1954. Print. ISBN 978-0-674-99444-7 | Ad Herennium, III. CCII. 36-XXIII. 38, pg 221

(8) http://classics.mit.edu/Aristotle/memory.html | On Memory and Reminiscence. By Aristotle
Written 350 B.C.E. Translated by J. I. Beare

(9) http://classics.mit.edu/Aristotle/memory.html | On Memory and Reminiscence. By Aristotle
Written 350 B.C.E. Translated by J. I. Beare

(10) We shall discuss these "fixed places" in greater detail later in the book. Generally, we refer to them as *backgrounds*.

(11) Ramon Llull, Local memory | MS Urb. Lat. 852, ff. 333r.-v., 334v., 338r. and 339v.: 'Localis memoria per Raimundum Lullum From Rossi, Paolo. *Logic and the Art of Memory: The Quest for a Universal Language.* Trans. Clucas, Stephen Chicago: The Athlone Press and the University of Chicago, 2000.Print.Pg 54,55 ISBN 0-226-72826-9

(12) Bruno, Giordano. *On the Composition of Images, Signs & Ideas,* 1591. Trans. Charles Doria. New York: Willis, Locker & Owens, 1991. Print. ISBN 0-930279-18-2

(13) Bruno, Giordano. *On the Composition of Images, Signs & Ideas,* 1591. Trans. Charles Doria. New York: Willis, Locker & Owens, 1991. Print. ISBN 0-930279-18-2

(14) Aristotle. *The Categories on Interpretation.* Trans. P. Cooke, Harold. London: Harvard University Press. Print. Pg 17-18. ISBN 978-0-674-99359-4

(15) I have added this one topic because it seemed reasonable to do so, but this is not one of Aristotle's. It is not included in the table for that reason.

(16) Aristotle. *Topics.* Trans. S. Forster, E. London: Harvard University Press. Print. ISBN 978-0-674-99430-0 | Pg 19

(17) (μ is the Greek letter Mu, which sounds a lot like a cow)

(18) The New Art of Memory Founded Upon the Principles Taught by M Gregor Von Feinaigle | PIBN 1000749489 | pg 341-343, Dr. Grey's System, Fourth edition of the Memoria Technica

(19) In this work, the author choice to denote a background by the word "symbol." It has herein been replaced according the particular terminology of this work; they have the same meaning.

(20) The New Art of Memory Founded Upon the Principles Taught by M Gregor Von Feinaigle | PIBN 1000749489

(21) The New Art of Memory Founded Upon the Principles Taught by M Gregor Von Feinaigle | PIBN 1000749489 | Chapter on Poetry and Prose. Pg 163 – 166

(22) Peter of Ravenna, Phoenix seu artificiosa memoria, ff.88v., 89r. | Rossi, Paolo. *Logic and the Art of Memory: The Quest for a Universal Language.* Trans. Clucas, Stephen Chicago: The Athlone Press and the University of Chicago, 2000. Print. ISBN 0-226-72826-9

(23) Rossi, Paolo. *Logic and the Art of Memory: The Quest for a Universal Language.* Trans. Clucas, Stephen Chicago: The Athlone Press and the University of Chicago, 2000. Print. | ISBN 0-226-72826-9 | pg 53 | Ramon Llull, Combinatoria | Munich, Staatsbibliotek, MS 10593, f. 3r.-v

(24) Cicero. *Rhetorica ad Herennium.* Trans. Caplan, Harry. London, England. Harvard University Press. 1954. Print. ISBN 978-0-674-99444-7 | Ad Herennium, III. XXIV. 39-40, pg 225